WIN-WIN

AN EVERYDAY GUIDE
TO NEGOTIATING

WIN-WIN

DAVID GOLDWICH

Marshall Cavendish
Business

Published by Marshall Cavendish Business
An imprint of Marshall Cavendish International

A member of the
Times Publishing Group

Other Marshall Cavendish Offices:
Marshall Cavendish Corporation, 800 Westchester Ave, Suite N-641, Rye Brook,
NY 10573, USA • Marshall Cavendish International (Thailand) Co Ltd, 253 Asoke,
16th Floor, Sukhumvit 21 Road, Klongtoey Nua, Wattana, Bangkok 10110, Thailand •
Marshall Cavendish (Malaysia) Sdn Bhd, Times Subang, Lot 46, Subang Hi-Tech
Industrial Park, Batu Tiga, 40000 Shah Alam, Selangor Darul Ehsan, Malaysia

Marshall Cavendish is a registered trademark of Times Publishing Limited

National Library Board, Singapore Cataloguing in Publication Data

Name(s): Goldwich, David, 1959-
Title: Win-win : an everyday guide to negotiating / David Goldwich.
Description: Singapore : Marshall Cavendish Business, [2020]
Identifier(s): OCN 1145819419 | ISBN 978-981-48-6853-2 (paperback)
Subject(s): LCSH: Negotiation in business. | Negotiation.
Classification: DDC 658.4052--dc23

Printed in Singapore

CONTENTS

INTRODUCTION

We all negotiate every day, whether we realize it or not. Yet few people ever learn *how* to negotiate. Those who do usually learn the traditional, win-lose negotiating style rather than an approach that is likely to result in a win-win agreement. This old-school, adversarial approach may be useful in a one-off negotiation where you will probably not deal with that party again. However, such transactions are becoming increasingly rare, because most of us deal with the same people repeatedly—our spouses and children, our friends and colleagues, our customers and clients. In view of this, it's essential to achieve successful results for ourselves and maintain a healthy relationship with our negotiating partners at the same time. In today's interdependent world of business partnerships and long-term relationships, a win-win outcome is fast becoming the *only* acceptable result.

While we hear much talk about the coveted win-win outcome, this result is actually not common. Most negotiations will never result in a win-win outcome because of certain common negotiation mistakes and misconceptions. The win-lose mindset is so pervasive that it seems natural for many people. In this book, I hope to change this perception.

Win-win negotiators value their business and social relationships. They know that winning in a given negotiation is not as important as maintaining their winning relationships. Yet this does not mean that they must sacrifice their interests. Win-win negotiators believe they can win both the negotiation and the relationship. Most importantly, they understand that they can consistently achieve win-win results by developing and using a set of win-win negotiating skills and techniques.

Some people who attend negotiation seminars hope to learn the secret to being a master negotiator. Unfortunately, there is no secret. There is only a body of guidelines, principles, strategies, tactics, and skills to learn and practice. There is also psychology and an understanding of human behavior. And, of course, there are communication and interpersonal skills. None of these is a magic bullet. You must practice and improve in all of these areas.

As you become more adept, your negotiated outcomes will improve. Sometimes, you will find that one masterstroke makes a huge difference. More often, you will use a combination of skills to make incremental improvements in your negotiating ability. For example, many of my students are amazed to find that by learning one simple technique—such as making a more aggressive first offer or counter-offer than they normally would—they can achieve better outcomes in all of their negotiations.

You can study negotiation for the rest of your life. On the plus side, you can also reap the benefits of these improved outcomes for the rest of your life. Given that you negotiate every day, this can add up to a fantastic sum. So play the game and have fun! Perhaps there *is* a secret after all—*Preparation*. Most people do not prepare much for a negotiation, and many do not prepare at all. Do you see an opportunity here?

You too can develop the win-win negotiator's mindset and learn the skills and techniques to successfully negotiate win-win agreements. The fact that you are reading these lines shows that you are interested in becoming a better negotiator—a win-win negotiator. As you continue reading, you will come to appreciate the benefits of the win-win mindset. You will find that the tools you need are not difficult to master. And you will realize that negotiating can be both fun and rewarding. Negotiation isn't just for lawyers and wheeler-dealers, it's for everybody, including you.

I hope you'll practice the skills and techniques shared in this book, and enjoy your journey towards becoming a win-win negotiator.

David Goldwich
www.davidgoldwich.com

CHAPTER 1

PREPARING TO NEGOTIATE

"The man who is prepared has his battle half fought."
— Cervantes

"The general who wins the battle makes many calculations in his temple before the battle is fought. The general who loses makes but few calculations beforehand."
— Sun Tzu

East or West, it's the same idea: Preparation is key.

WHAT IS NEGOTIATION?

We all negotiate every day, often without realizing that's what we're doing. We negotiate with our bosses and colleagues, our spouses and children, our customers and clients, people we sell to and people we buy from. We negotiate prices, goods, services, activities, schedules, terms, incentives, and relationships.

You probably have some idea about what negotiation is. Even without a formal definition, we know it when we see it. Negotiation is a way of satisfying your interests, of getting what you need or want. We live in a complicated world and don't have the time, skill, or inclination to do everything ourselves.

We rely on others to help us. Similarly, others approach us to help satisfy their own interests. Negotiation is the process that facilitates these exchanges.

Imagine it's "bring your child to work" day. Your daughter is sitting quietly in your office, playing with her iPad. You say, "We're going to a negotiation. Just sit quietly and don't interrupt." The kid is thinking, "A negotiation? That sounds important, I wonder what it is?" At dinner that evening, your wife asks her, "How did you like going to the office with daddy?"

Your daughter replies, "We went to a negotiation!"

"Oh, that sounds exciting! What was it like?"

"It was so boring! All they did was talk the whole time!"

At the most basic level, negotiation is a form of persuasive communication. It is a way of getting others to do what we want them to do. As such, it requires us to use all of our communication skills: listening, asking questions, sharing information, interpreting information, framing proposals, reading body language, influencing, and persuading. It requires empathy and understanding, knowledge and insight, diplomacy and tact.

When I ask my students what negotiation is, I get the same answers almost every time:

- It's getting what you want.
- Two or more people interacting to reach an agreement.
- A means to satisfy your interests with the help of another.
- Give and take to make a deal.
- Compromise.
- Bargaining.
- Getting as much as you can for as little as possible.
- Getting a win-win.

While all of these may be part of the big picture of negotiation, I like to think of it in other ways.

Negotiation is an exercise in joint problem solving. Why am I negotiating? Because I have a problem or need that I cannot satisfy on my own. I need a widget. Why would my negotiating counterpart bother to negotiate with me? Because she also has a problem. She has a warehouse full of widgets that she needs to sell. Two people, two problems. And how do we approach our counterpart? We think: "I had better keep my cards close to my chest, give her as little information as possible or she will use it against me somehow, maybe even mislead her for my own advantage." And she's probably thinking the same thing! How can we solve our problems with all that secrecy and deception?

Consider taking the joint problem-solving approach. Two people, two points of view, two sources of ideas, working together to solve one problem: how do we reach an agreement that best satisfies our interests? If both parties can look at negotiation as a shared problem and strive to solve it together, they are both more likely to satisfy their own interests.

Unfortunately, this is not the way most people approach negotiation, but my purpose in writing this book is to help you change that mindset and become a win-win negotiator.

Negotiation is a process. Many people tend to think of negotiation as an event—bargaining—where we sit at a table with someone, playing the negotiation game, trying to satisfy our own interests through various machinations or perhaps by engaging in enlightened collaborative problem solving. The truth is that the process of negotiation begins sooner than we think. *It begins as soon as we recognize a need that we cannot satisfy on our own, and we set out to reach an agreement with someone who can help us satisfy that need.* At this point, we may have not even identified a negotiating counterpart, we have merely identified a need. We begin the process of negotiation by clarifying our true interests and thinking about possible ways to satisfy them.

Negotiation is a game. Like the box of a board game says, "For two or more players." Like other games, the negotiation game has some rules, though there are a lot more guidelines than firm rules. There are strategies and tactics you can learn, as well as counter-tactics for every tactic. Negotiation is a game of skill and chance. The more skill you have, the less you are at the mercy of chance. And like most games, there are winners and losers, but a good negotiation well played can leave everyone a winner.

Like most games, negotiation is meant to be fun. It may not feel like fun, because we feel pressure to get a good result and so we take it too seriously. But fun is in the mind of the player. With the right mindset, negotiation can be a lot of fun and very rewarding.

WHY DO WE NEGOTIATE?

We negotiate because we want something that we cannot get on our own. Someone else is in a position to give it to us or can help us get it. Alternatively, someone may be in a position to harm our interests, and we seek to dissuade them from doing so. In other words, we negotiate with a counterpart because they can help us or hurt us.

From this perspective, we are dependent on someone else. We feel weak, needy, and at their mercy. We see our counterpart as having power over us.

What we may not see is that our counterpart also wants something from us, or he wouldn't be negotiating with us. We do not see how weak and powerless he feels as he deals with us, because he dare not show it. It's important to remember that we are also in a position to affect his interests in a positive or negative way. He may need us as much as we need him.

Consequently, we find ourselves in a web of relationships and interdependencies. We all need things from others, and we turn to one another for help. Negotiation is the process by which we help each other get what we need.

THE NEGOTIATION PROCESS

I mentioned earlier that while negotiation is usually thought of as an event, it is in fact a process. This process begins the moment you perceive a want or need and set out to satisfy it. At that point, you may not even be thinking about negotiating. You may not realize you are negotiating until you are actually bargaining with someone over how much it will cost you to meet that need. By then it is too late—your counterpart knows you need him and he knows you are unprepared. You've lost.

Stage 1: Preparation

In *The Art of War*, the Chinese military strategist Sun Tzu wrote, "If you know the enemy and know yourself, you need not fear the result of a hundred battles." In other words, preparation is the key to victory in battle. The same can be said of negotiation.

So how do you prepare for a negotiation? Most people who are preparing to negotiate to buy something will have in mind a very low price that they would love to pay, the highest price they are willing to pay, and a figure in the middle of that range, representing an estimate of what they expect to end up paying. Sellers go through a similar exercise. It's good to think about these expectations, but it is not enough.

You may imagine yourself a big shot negotiator and think you can just wing it, but understand this: real big shot negotiators do not wing it, they prepare. Here are some considerations to bear in mind as you prepare:

- Know thyself. What do you want? Not what you *think* you want, but what you *really* want. Surprisingly, many people are unsure of this. For example, you may think you want a raise in salary, and perhaps you do. But you might really want something else, such as recognition, to be treated fairly, to maintain or improve your standard of living, or to provide security for your future. A pay raise might do it, but there might be other ways of meeting your needs.

- Once you've determined what you want—or what you think you want—ask yourself why you want it. After asking yourself why a few times, you may realize you need something else after all. You cannot achieve a satisfactory outcome in a negotiation until you are clear about your real interests and goals, that is, what you want or need, and why you want or need it.

- You will often find that you have multiple interests. You need to prioritize these. For example, in negotiating a position with a new employer, you might be interested in many things other than salary, such as insurance plans and other benefits, a flexible schedule, work environment, work assignments, team assignments, and so on. Some of these will be more important to you than others. It is unlikely that you will get everything you want. Prioritize your wish list into those items you must have, those you are willing to bargain for, and those that would be nice but not necessary. Then focus on your priorities and avoid being distracted by minor issues.

- Assess what resources you have, what you bring to the table. What do you have that your counterpart might want? List everything, tangible (money, products, service) and intangible (brand, reputation, emotional needs). These assets or bargaining chips—anything of value that you might offer to exchange—are called currencies of exchange, or simply currencies. How can you present these currencies to justify your demands?

• What strategies and tactics might you employ in the negotiation? Will you make the first offer, or wait for the other party to do so? What concessions are you willing to make, and when? What is your time frame? What is your walk-away point? What is your Plan B?

All of this is a lot to think about, but we're not done yet! There are many other things you must consider:

• Know the other party. Learn what you can about her from LinkedIn and other online sources, as well as from people you know who may know her. What does she want from you? Is she clear about her interests? What are her priorities? Does she really want what she says she wants, or does she have a hidden agenda? What is her backup plan if she doesn't reach an agreement with you? What intangible or emotional considerations might be motivating her?

• Anticipate your counterpart's negotiating style. Will he be a tough adversary or a collaborating partner? What is his negotiating strategy, and what tactics might he employ?

• Formulate some options. Based on your knowledge of what you want, the currencies you have, and your understanding of your counterpart's interests, begin putting together some options. An option is a package of currencies—a possible solution to your negotiating problem. Create some options that will satisfy your interests as well as your counterpart's. Be prepared to present these options and discuss them.

- Assess your alternatives. If you cannot ultimately reach an agreement with your counterpart, how will you satisfy your interests? What is your Plan B? If you do not have a backup plan, you are not ready to negotiate.

- Know the environment. You and your counterpart will not negotiate in a vacuum. You will both be influenced by various factors. Some of these you can control, others you can only anticipate or respond to. The more you know about them, the better your prospects. Learn as much as you can about the subject of your negotiation, your industry and business environment, and your counterpart.

- Consider how events in the political or economic space might affect you or your counterpart. Are there any relevant changes or trends in your respective industries? What government policies or regulations might have an impact on the negotiation? Does your counterpart have a business cycle you should know about? For example, car sales at the end of the month or toy sales before Christmas might provide an opportunity for you.

You can see that there is a lot to take into account before you negotiate. Gathering information is crucial in preparing for a negotiation. With all of the information available online, you can learn a great deal before you even introduce yourself to a counterpart. But you can also glean useful information from your counterpart.

Stage 2: Laying the foundation

Never begin a negotiation by making or soliciting an offer. Save that for later. First you need to lay a foundation with your counterpart. Get to know them. Make small talk. Build rapport. Present yourself as likable. Let them get comfortable with you.

Ask questions. Try to learn about them, their needs, and their situation. A simple question such as "How's business?" not only breaks the ice, but can get you useful information. If they reply, "Things have been slow lately," wouldn't that be good to know?

Try to get a sense of what they want. Are they knowledgeable and prepared, or trying to wing it? Are they more focused on price or reliability? Do they have any constraints, such as timing, budget, or other concerns?

Check your assumptions by asking the same questions in different forms. Are their answers consistent? Are you learning anything new? Continually reassess the value of information as you move into the bargaining phase and throughout the negotiation.

Stage 3: Bargaining

After gathering information and preparing to negotiate, you will move to the main event: bargaining. This is what most people think of as negotiating. It may involve face-to-face discussions, phone calls, e-mail exchanges, and even text messages. You and your counterpart will make offers and counter-offers, employ tactics and counter-tactics, explore options, make concessions, test assumptions, clarify understandings, and probably encounter one or more deadlocks throughout the negotiation.

During the bargaining phase, you will encounter new information that will force you to reassess what you thought you had learned in the preparation and laying the foundation stages. This is normal. Treat information gathered during these early stages as part of a working hypothesis. A good negotiator is open-minded enough to accept that some of his original ideas were wrong, and flexible enough to learn and adapt along the way.

Just remember that the formal bargaining event is only *part* of the negotiation process. If you think the negotiation begins and ends with bargaining and you did not put in the effort during stages one and two (preparation and laying the foundation), you have probably already lost. Do not confuse the grand finale—the handshake, the signing of the contract—with the work, research, and preparation that gets you there.

Stage 4: Closing the deal
Hopefully, as a result of all this work, you will reach an agreement that satisfies your interests as fully as possible. Even so, you are not done yet. In a formal business negotiation, you will need to document the terms in a formal agreement. You will need to anticipate what might go wrong as you implement the agreement and protect against these deal breakers. This may be the last thing you feel like doing after a protracted negotiation—you'd much rather celebrate your success and bask in the warm afterglow.

And you might be able to do that—if you have a lawyer or PA to tie up all the loose ends. Otherwise, it's on you. Agreements don't execute themselves, and most business agreements are not fully implemented. How unfortunate, when you consider that the whole point of business is to make things happen.

What if a dispute over the terms arises later on? Are you going to call your lawyer, spend a fortune on legal fees, and sabotage your business relationship with your counterpart while waiting for a judge to decide your case two years down the road? Or will you provide for some dispute resolution mechanism to streamline the process?

What if you later think of a way to improve on your agreement? Will you smack yourself in the head and say, "Oh well, too late now"? Or will you ask to renegotiate or propose a Post-Settlement Settlement?

We've all seen that silly sign on the wall of an office somewhere: "The job isn't finished until the paperwork is done!"

THE NEGOTIATING ENVIRONMENT

Negotiation does not take place in isolation. The environment can have an impact on the process. I have met people who manipulated the environment in devious ways. One client told me he would make the room so cold his counterpart would agree to almost anything just to get out! Another would schedule negotiations in mid-afternoon and seat his counterpart facing the window, where the glare of the sun was intense. You don't have to be so sneaky, but you should consider how the physical environment can affect the dynamics of a negotiation.

Venue

When it comes to the venue there are few rules, only guidelines. A good negotiator will consider all of these variables before deciding on an appropriate venue that will set the stage for the formal bargaining phase of the negotiation:

- Where should the negotiation take place? In your office or theirs? You may like the feeling of confidence and control that comes with the home field advantage, where you can choose the room and the seating arrangements and can manipulate the environment to project the image you desire. You also have your colleagues to back you up, as well as the administrative support of your staff.

- You may prefer to meet your counterpart in their own surroundings, where they feel more comfortable. This gives them the illusion of control. It gives you the opportunity to observe them on their own turf and draw inferences about them. For example, does their organization run smoothly or do they seem to be in disarray? What does the environment say about their financial condition and their ability to spend?

- You may choose to meet on neutral territory, such as a restaurant or a hotel conference room. Meeting on neutral ground would help mitigate the effects of a home field advantage, and can also take you away from the distractions of your office. Would a formal or casual setting work better for you? Many business deals are sealed on the golf course, not in the boardroom.

Seating

There is a reason why round tables are used whenever heads of state meet at an international summit—there is no head of a round table, so everyone appears equal. However, most corporate conference rooms have long tables, with a head and a foot. The head, obviously, is the power seat. It is reserved for the captain of the home team, and adds to his authority. You want your counterpart to sit at the head of his table and feel in control. Do *not* sit at the head of his table yourself, unless you think challenging your counterpart is a useful tactic.

What if you are sitting at a smaller table? Sitting opposite your counterpart at a table suggests an adversarial dynamic. After all, we play chess, table tennis, and other competitive games from opposite sides of a table. Sitting side by side, or kitty-corner, suggests both parties are attacking a problem together, from a common perspective. This sends a more positive message. It is even better if the table is round. Better still, consider sitting informally on a sofa or chairs around a coffee table (though not directly opposite one another) as this more relaxed setting may help the parties loosen up and speak freely.

SETTING THE AGENDA

Develop an agenda before you sit down with your counterpart. The agenda should reflect the items to be discussed and their relative importance. Start with smaller or easier items to establish a pattern of success. Use this momentum to help carry you through the more difficult points.

Ideally, you should create the agenda yourself. Your counterpart may appreciate you taking on this extra work. It also gives you some control over the negotiation.

If your counterpart prepares an agenda, review it carefully to make sure it works for you. Keep in mind that it may have been crafted to give him certain advantages. If you see anything you would like to modify, suggest a change, and offer a reason for it. Everything is negotiable—even the agenda!

Watch out if the other party tries to deviate from the agenda during the negotiation. It's easy to lose track of items that are taken out of order.

Make notes on your copy of the agenda to aid your memory later. Even with the best of intentions, you may forget a detail or the context of a discussion. Use your annotated agenda as the basis for a memorandum that you will draft shortly after the session.

SHOULD YOU BRING A TEAM?

It's a good idea to bring a team, or at least one other person, to a negotiation whenever possible. Solo negotiators generally achieve substantially less favorable outcomes than those who negotiate as part of a team. Most people tend to perform better when others are backing them up, giving them confidence, and depending on them. Also, when you have others around, you have the benefit of multiple sources of experience, talent, and perspective. Two (or more) heads are always better than one.

Having a partner with you also allows you to use the good guy/ bad guy tactic, which we will consider in Chapter 7. It also gives you a psychological edge.

However, do not bring your whole team. You will not be able to limit your authority if all the decision makers are present. Leave yourself an out by making sure there is a higher authority not involved in the negotiation whom you will need to consult for final approval. This higher authority could be your accountant, your operations manager, or simply your "people."

What if your counterpart has a team and you don't? That could be intimidating, but it shouldn't be. Negotiation is a voluntary process, and you don't have to agree to anything that is not in your interests. Be confident in knowing that you are prepared, and remember that they need you as much as you need them. And take heart in the knowledge that solo negotiators can still achieve good results. A deal can be either good or bad regardless of how many people are in the room.

YOU'RE NOT JUST NEGOTIATING WITH HIM

Most negotiators focus on the person sitting across the table from them. They may even tailor their words and approach to this person's personality, negotiating style, and other individual characteristics. This sounds good, but it isn't enough. The person you're looking at is often just the tip of the iceberg.

There's more to consider than just the person sitting at the table with you. Your counterpart has other constituents to answer to.

He will need to gain their buy-in. For example, his boss will be interested in the outcome, and he will be concerned about what his boss will think. You will have to justify your proposals to your counterpart, and help him justify his actions to his stakeholders. Try to identify who these stakeholders are, what their interests are, and how you can win their support.

Consider your counterpart negotiating a purchase from you. His boss is concerned about the price. Your counterpart is concerned about his boss. If you want him to agree to a higher price, help him justify to himself and his boss why your product is worth more. Help make him a hero in his boss' eyes.

THE WIN-WIN NEGOTIATOR'S CHECKLIST

In negotiation, as in so many other areas of life, preparation is the key to success. At the end of this book you will find the Win-Win Negotiator's Checklist. This checklist will help you prepare for all of your future negotiations, laying out the main points you need to consider from beginning to end. I mention it here because it is a crucial part of your preparation for any negotiation.

We have touched on some of the more important aspects of preparing for a win-win negotiation. In the next chapter, we will build on this foundation and explore the mindset of the win-win negotiator.

CHAPTER 2

THE WIN-WIN MINDSET

*"You can get everything in life you want, if you will
just help enough other people get what they want."*
— Zig Ziglar

WHY YOU NEED TO BE A WIN-WIN NEGOTIATOR

Most successful people in business learned how to negotiate
on the job. They would have gone to a few meetings with their
boss and watched her in action, then they would have taken
the lead in the next few meetings as their boss sat back and
watched, and after a few of those meetings the boss would
have said, "Congratulations, you are now a negotiator!" and
left them to their own devices. Where did the boss learn to
negotiate? From her boss, who learned from his boss, and so
on, all the way back to the days of the cavemen. The art was
passed down over centuries, but it was not the art of win-win
negotiation, it was an adversarial, old-school, win-lose style of
negotiating, sometimes called distributive, zero sum, or fixed
pie negotiation.

Win-lose negotiators see negotiation as a pie to be divided, and
they want the bigger slice. In other words, one person will win

and the other will lose, so they do their best to win. How do they know when they have won? They see they have the bigger slice of the pie, or that their counterpart looks beaten. A loss for the other party is interpreted as a win for them.

This win-lose approach is only suitable for one-time transactions, where in all likelihood you will never see the other party again. In this situation, you probably don't really care if the other guy loses. You might care, though, if you believe in fairness, or karma, or if you want to maintain a good reputation in a world that is getting smaller and more interconnected by the day. In an isolated instance, however, most people just want to win.

Throughout most of history the win-lose approach was the norm. Our caveman ancestors lived or died by the law of the jungle, eat or be eaten. But isolated, one-off negotiations are now the exception. Most of us must negotiate with the same people repeatedly over a long period of time: colleagues, customers, vendors, and partners. We need to achieve good results for our side while maintaining a healthy, long-term relationship with our negotiating partners. In today's world, a win-win outcome is fast becoming the only acceptable result.

Take a look at your computer. Aside from the manufacturer's brand, there are probably two or three other logos stamped onto the casing, such as Intel or Microsoft. When Intel and the computer manufacturer negotiate the price of computer chips, do you think either company would accept a win-lose result? Of course not! Both parties have lots of money, resources, expertise, and talent. They also have a long-term relationship that is more important than the outcome of any one of their many negotiations. Neither would accept a loss. They must both have a win-win result.

I suspect that you too would like to have a win-win agreement in most, if not all, of your negotiations. With the tips found in this book, your chances of negotiating win-win outcomes will increase exponentially.

Some wag once said this about the weather: everyone talks about it but no one does anything about it. That's one of the first things that comes to my mind when I hear someone talk about a win-win outcome in a negotiation. Everyone says they want it, but very few people are able to achieve it with any regularity. In fact, few people even understand what it is.

A win-win is not just reaching an agreement. Nor is it a favorable outcome, or when both parties feel they have won. That is usually a partial win at best. A true win-win is when both parties get the best possible deal without leaving anything on the table. It is not just acceptable, it is *optimal*.

The elusive win-win is not easy to achieve, but you can learn how to increase the odds in your favor.

Win-win negotiators are found in the same places as win-lose and lose-lose negotiators. They are not any more experienced, and they look about the same as well. The big difference between win-win negotiators and all the others is their mindset.

Win-win negotiators understand the five styles of negotiating and are able to adapt to their counterpart's style and to the situation. They choose to exhibit certain positive behaviors and avoid negative ones. They are optimistic, open-minded, and collaborate with their negotiating partner to solve their problems together. In this chapter, we will explore the mindset of a win-win negotiator.

POSSIBLE OUTCOMES

In any negotiation there are several possible outcomes:

- **Win-lose**

  One party wins, and the other loses. This can happen when the parties are mismatched, or when one party is not prepared. It can also result from cheating. In any case, the loser will resent the winner, and any relationship between the parties will suffer. Still, we would all rather win than lose, and it is easy to see how this result could come about.

- **Lose-lose**

  Both parties lose. You may be thinking, "How can that be? It's easy to see how one party might lose, but how can both parties voluntarily agree to lose? It just isn't rational!" You're right, it isn't rational. It is, however, surprisingly easy to become emotional in a negotiation, and one may agree to lose so long as he takes the other person down with him. In addition, much depends on how you define "lose." You might see a suicide bombing as a lose-lose, but the terrorist sees it as a win for him.

- **Partial win-partial lose**

  This is by far the most common negotiating outcome. Both parties get part of what they want, but neither has his interests fully satisfied. This seems fair since both come out better off than they were, and we all understand that we can't realistically expect to get everything we want. Or can we?

- **Win-win**

  Both parties get everything they want! This is the best of all possible worlds! It's the ideal outcome. But while the win-win is much talked about, much sought after, and much prized, it is rarely achieved. The main purpose of this book is to help make this outcome easier to achieve.

FIVE STYLES OF NEGOTIATING

There are two dimensions that determine negotiating style: assertiveness and people orientation.

Assertiveness is the ability to communicate your interests clearly and directly. It means standing up for yourself without stepping on anyone else's toes. Assertive people are able to ask for what they want, say no when they need to, and state how they feel in any situation. They also accept standards of fairness and recognize the rights and interests of others. They are able to advance their own interests without guilt or reservation.

People orientation denotes a sensitivity to the needs and feelings of others. It encompasses empathy, emotional awareness, and ease in social situations. Those with a high people orientation

THE WIN-WIN MINDSET 33

are generally sociable and likable. They are people driven rather than task driven, and they seek to understand their counterpart's interests as well as their own.

Your negotiating style is a function of how assertive and how people oriented you are, as illustrated in this diagram:

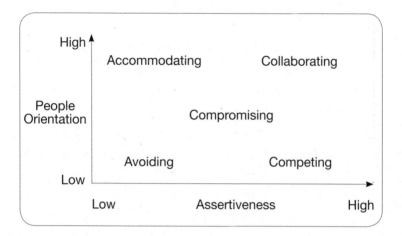

1. Avoiding

A person with an avoiding style of negotiating avoids the issues, the other party, and negotiation situations as much as possible. An avoiding negotiator

- avoids confrontation, controversy, tense situations,
- avoids discussing issues, concerns—especially sensitive ones,
- is uncomfortable asserting her needs and saying no to her counterpart, and
- puts off negotiating whenever possible.

2. **Accommodating**

The accommodating negotiator is primarily concerned with preserving his relationship with the other party, even at the expense of his own substantive interests. An accommodating negotiator

- is uncomfortable saying no and focuses on the other party's concerns more than his own,
- helps the other party at his own expense,
- tries to win approval by pleasing the other party,
- follows the other party's lead, and
- emphasizes areas of agreement and downplays or ignores differences.

3. **Competing**

The competing style of negotiating is characterized by an emphasis on self-interest and winning at the other party's expense. A competitive negotiator

- uses power to effect a more favorable outcome,
- exploits the other party's weaknesses,
- wears the other party down until he gives in, and
- may use threats, manipulation, dishonesty, and hardball tactics.

4. **Compromising**

The compromising style places a premium on fairness and balance, with each party making some sacrifice to get part of what they want. A compromising negotiator believes she is unlikely to get everything she wants and

- is quick to split the difference,
- assumes a quid pro quo, give-and-take process is necessary, and

- seeks a solution in the middle of the range, without making much effort to find a win-win outcome.

5. **Collaborating**

Negotiators with a collaborating style seek an optimal outcome by focusing on mutual interests and trying to satisfy each other's needs. A collaborating negotiator

- deals openly and communicates clearly and effectively,
- builds trust,
- listens to the other party,
- shares ideas and information,
- seeks understanding and creative solutions,
- considers multiple options,
- strives to create value, and
- sees negotiating as an exercise in joint problem solving.

Avoiding and accommodating negotiators generally do not fare well in negotiations, especially when their counterpart has a stronger style. They tend to be soft and are not comfortable being firm. They need to be more assertive. Preparing thoroughly may help compensate for their lack of confidence and drive at the negotiating table. This means understanding the subject matter, their interests and currencies, and their counterparts' interests, currencies, needs, and constraints. It also means anticipating what might occur during the negotiation and having a clear idea of what they will do if various contingencies unfold. Having an assertive colleague present during negotiating sessions could also help, as people often push harder for others than for themselves, but I strongly recommend a course on assertiveness training and practice developing assertiveness skills.

Competitive negotiators look for a win-lose result—winning is everything. It would be wise for them to help their counterpart get at least a partial win as well. After all, they still win, and they also gain goodwill by allowing their counterpart to enjoy a better than expected outcome. However, competitive negotiators often *want* to see their counterpart lose: for them, it reinforces the idea that they have won. It is not pleasant dealing with a competitive negotiator, even if you are assertive. However, you will need to negotiate with such a person on occasion. The best you can do is to understand him, brace yourself, and try to find a win-win. He may not begrudge you a win if he wins as well, but ultimately, he is only concerned with his own interests.

Compromising negotiators, at first glance, appear reasonable. They are willing to give up something in exchange for something else, provided their counterparts do the same. It seems only fair. Some people even define negotiation as the art of compromise. However, this approach does the art of negotiating a disservice. As we will see shortly, it is the easy way out. It is far better to learn the ways of the win-win negotiator than to settle for a quick and easy partial win.

Collaborating negotiators, as you have probably guessed, are win-win negotiators. They work with their counterparts to solve their problem together by building trust, communicating openly, identifying interests, leveraging currencies, and designing options that allow them to create maximum value for all involved.

THE WIN-WIN MINDSET 37

WHEN TO USE EACH STYLE

The collaborating style of negotiating is clearly the win-win approach. If we are advocating the win-win approach and learning win-win techniques, why bother with the other four styles? There are a few reasons.

- While you may be sold on the merits of win-win negotiating, your counterpart may not see it that way. You will find yourself dealing with competitive types. You need to recognize that style and know how to protect yourself.

- Even committed win-win negotiators can use other styles. Sometimes you will be expected to be competitive, or to compromise. Remember, negotiation is a game. You need to understand and play by the rules.

- No single style is good enough for all occasions. You will need to be flexible enough to adopt other styles.

- And let's face it, there may be times when you adopt a competitive posture because you want to win as much as possible and are not concerned with how your counterpart fares. When buying a used car or negotiating disputed charges with the phone company, do you really care if the other party doesn't make money on the deal?

Most people have a dominant or preferred style, but it may vary with the situation and the people involved. While collaboration is generally the best outcome, and avoidance and accommodation are not usually effective, there are times when each style has its own advantages.

Consider choosing an approach based on the following factors:

1. **Avoiding**

   When the issue is trivial, it may not be worth your time. When emotions are running high, it is wise to put off negotiating until the emotions subside. However, this should be a temporary measure. Avoidance is a poor long-term strategy. If you find yourself rationalizing avoiding behavior frequently, face reality and sign up for assertiveness training.

2. **Accommodating**

   When the issue in question is not important to you but is important to the other party, you may choose to let them have the point. This is an easy concession to make in exchange for something else later. You might ask for something on the spot in exchange for your concession. Or you might just bask in the magnanimity of letting the other person have what they want, especially if the relationship is a close one (like a marriage!).

3. **Competing**

   In a one-off negotiation where you have no ongoing relationship with your counterpart, you may not care whether he wins or loses, you just want a win. Or in a negotiation where the only issue is price, a gain for one party means a loss for the other. The most likely result when negotiating solely on price is a partial win for both parties, but you may want your part to be as big as possible. Finally, you may find yourself negotiating in a crisis situation that requires quick, decisive action on your part.

4. **Compromising**

   You may find yourself in a situation where time pressures require a prompt settlement, and you don't have the time to explore win-win solutions. Or where both parties are equal in power and neither will concede much. Or where the parties accept a compromise as a temporary measure to a complex problem, and intend to pursue a more lasting settlement later—for example, a ceasefire agreement rather than a full-blown treaty. You might also compromise when neither party can propose a win-win solution and both prefer a partial win to no deal, although in such cases it would be best to put in more effort and try to come up with more imaginative options.

5. **Collaborating**

   When both parties want a win-win and have the time and mindset to pursue it, the chance of a win-win is good. Or the issue may be too important to compromise, and failure is not an option. When a win-win is imperative, there is often a way to get it.

While collaboration is the ideal, even win-win negotiators need to use other approaches on occasion.

DISTRIBUTIVE VS INTEGRATIVE NEGOTIATIONS

Another factor that could influence your choice of negotiating style is whether the negotiation is a distributive or an integrative negotiation.

In a distributive, zero sum, or fixed pie negotiation, the parties negotiate over a single issue. To use a time-worn metaphor, this is about dividing the pie, and each party wants the bigger piece. Any gain by one party comes at the expense of the other. A win-lose or partial win result is likely, and some compromise is usually necessary.

The most common form of a distributive negotiation is where the parties haggle over the price of a single item. The sole issue is the price to be paid: the buyer wants to pay less, while the seller wants to receive more. Other single issue negotiations might involve the allocation of a limited resource such as time, manpower, or use of equipment.

In a distributive negotiation you are likely to adopt a competitive approach. When both parties want more, they have to fight for it. This is especially true in a one-off negotiation, where there is no continuing relationship. In some relationships—such as a marriage or a workplace setting—you will still have a series of single issue, distributive negotiations. In such cases you will want to think twice about a competitive stance and consider tradeoffs to keep the relationship on an even keel.

In an integrative negotiation there are multiple issues. This allows for the possibility of tradeoffs, creating value, expanding the pie, and maybe even a win-win. A collaborative approach will make that win-win more likely. By introducing additional issues to a single-issue negotiation you can change it from distributive to integrative and increase the likelihood of a win-win.

In reality, most negotiations are a mix of distributive and integrative. After the parties collaborate to make the pie as big as possible and create maximum value, they stop playing nice and try to get as much as they can. When shifting from integrative (expanding the pie) to distributive mode (dividing the pie), you don't want to seem like a Jekyll and Hyde. The transition is smoother when you create value for both parties, empathize, and have a solid rationale to justify your claims.

THE PROBLEM WITH COMPROMISE

When two people can't quite close the gap and reach an agreement, it is common to compromise. One person might say "Let's just split the difference," or "Let's meet in the middle." He believes this is the fair thing to do, as each party is making a sacrifice and each is getting part of what he wants. While compromise may seem fair, it is not good negotiating.

The Old Testament tells a story about two women, each claiming to be the mother of an infant. The women approached King Solomon to resolve their dispute. He suggested that they cut the baby in half, knowing that the real mother would prefer to see her child alive with someone else than dead in her own arms. Sure enough, he was right—King Solomon was known for his wisdom, after all! Imagine if the two women *did* agree to split the baby. That would definitely have been a lose-lose outcome, but a compromise often is.

When we compromise, both parties make a sacrifice. While each gets something, neither gets everything he wants. Compromising usually leads to a partial win at best, never a win-win.

A better way is to consider more options and try to find a win-win. Sure, it takes more effort, but we often take the easy way out and compromise far too quickly, without really trying to find a win-win solution.

Consider compromising only as a last resort. While compromise is often used to resolve difficult negotiations, it is a cop-out. Exhaust all efforts to collaborate on a win-win outcome before taking the easy way out. It may take time, perseverance, creativity, and a good flow of communication, but the results will be worth it.

Some years ago, my wife and I were discussing where to go for our vacation. She wanted to go to Hawaii, and I wanted to go to Kyoto. How could we resolve our differences?

1. We could go to Hawaii one year and she would be happy and I would not be, then go to Kyoto the next year and I would be happy and she would not be. Not optimal.
2. She could go to Hawaii and I could go to Kyoto. Also not optimal, possibly grounds for divorce.
3. We could meet in the middle—compromise—and we would have ended up somewhere in the Pacific Ocean. Definitely not optimal.

In the end, we understood that where we thought we wanted to go was a *position*. The reasons we wanted to go there reflected our *interests*. (Positions and interests will be covered in the next chapter.) I asked her why she wanted to go to Hawaii. She gave her reasons:

1. "I like a relaxing vacation. Kyoto is not relaxing, it is hectic, getting on the tour bus, going to a shrine, getting off the tour bus to visit the shrine, getting back on the bus to go to the next shrine, etc."

2 "I like a tropical vacation with a beach. Kyoto is not tropical, and I don't think it has a beach."

3. "I like to enjoy a drink and watch the sunset. Kyoto is in the land of the rising sun, and I don't know if it has a sunset."

Then I gave her my reasons why I wanted to go to Kyoto:

1. "I am an art lover. Kyoto has a lot of great art. The only art in Hawaii are those carved coconut heads."

2. "I also appreciate architecture. Kyoto has magnificent architecture, with wooden temples hundreds of years old, built without a single nail. Hawaii's architecture is mostly uninspiring post-WWII cement block buildings."

3. "I like a place with a sense of history. Kyoto has an exceptionally rich history."

Having identified our interests, our task was to find a place that satisfied both of our interests to the greatest extent possible. Where could we go that was relaxing, had fabulous beaches and gorgeous sunsets, as well as a rich sense of history with lots of great art and architecture? We went to Bali, and we were both happy.

FRAMING

Two people can look at the same situation and interpret it differently. One sees the glass as half empty, the other as half full. One sees a risk, the other an opportunity. How you see it depends on the lens through which you view the world, or your frame.

A frame is an arbitrary reference point that influences the way a person views a situation. While people will usually adopt a frame without giving it much thought, they can be swayed to adopt another frame. This ability to shape another's perceptions is too powerful to ignore. Consequently, a win-win negotiator thinks about how issues are framed.

You may be familiar with the story of Tom Sawyer whitewashing his Aunt Polly's fence. One fine sunny morning, Aunt Polly assigned Tom this unpleasant chore. As Tom toiled away, other kids interrupted their play to tease him. Tom pretended not to be bothered, and told the others it wasn't *work*, it was *fun*. After all, you can go swimming or fishing anytime, but it's not every day you get the chance to whitewash a fence.

It wasn't long before the other boys were begging for a turn with the brush. Tom expressed doubt as to whether he should let others share in his fun, which made them even more eager to do it. Soon, all the boys in the neighborhood were lining up for a turn, and trading their prized possessions for the privilege! Tom relaxed in the shade, enjoying his windfall while the others completed his chore.

Tom Sawyer was able to persuade others to do an unpleasant task by framing it in a positive way. The other boys adopted his frame and agreed to his proposal.

Most people feel more strongly about avoiding a loss than working for a gain. In a widely cited study, Nobel Prize winner Daniel Kahneman and Amos Tversky found that people were motivated twice as much by the fear of a loss as by the prospect of a gain.* In other words, losing is twice as painful as winning is enjoyable. People in a loss-minimizing frame of mind will try harder and risk more to avoid the loss. You can exploit this mindset by playing to their fears, by saying, "It would be a shame to miss out on this deal after all we've put into it."

People in a gain maximizing frame, on the other hand, are more conservative and more likely to accept a moderate gain than to fight hard for a more advantageous settlement. They are easier to negotiate with. The upshot of all this is that you should encourage your counterpart to adopt a gain maximizing frame. You can influence her by emphasizing what she stands to gain if you are able to reach an agreement, rather than what she may lose if you don't. A frame emphasizing what you're giving the other party ("We can let you have the apartment for $1,600 a month") normally works better than one in which you're asking them to give up something ("We're asking $1,600 a month rent for the apartment").

---

* Daniel Kahneman and Amos Tversky, "Prospect Theory: An Analysis of Decision under Risk," *Econometrica*, 47(2), pp. 263–291, March 1979 and subsequent work.

When facing a possible gain, most people become more risk averse—our desire to hold onto our gain and not lose it is stronger than our desire to try to win more. Casino operators know this. Winners usually want to hang onto their winnings and quit. Losing gamblers will usually keep playing in the hopes of overcoming their loss. This approach works for the casinos because it's a numbers game for them—they don't have to know the risk appetite of every guest. But in the negotiation setting, it pays to know the risk profile of your individual counterpart and frame the issues accordingly.

It is also important to know your own risk profile and frame. A negative frame leads us to be less flexible, to offer fewer and smaller concessions, and to be less satisfied with the outcome and the process. It also makes us more prone to impasse and quicker to resort to litigation.

The best negotiators think about how to frame issues to their advantage. By framing an issue or wording a proposal a certain way, you can influence the way your counterpart responds. Do you advocate a proposal based on what the other party stands to gain by doing the deal, or what he will lose by not reaching an agreement? You can also frame issues in other ways, such as fair/unfair, popular/unique, traditional/cutting edge, and so on. Just remember that the frame needs to be believable, so be sure you are able to justify it. For example, in business we don't like to use us the word "problem"; we would rather frame it as a challenge or maybe even as an opportunity. But it would not have been believable for the Apollo 13 astronauts to say, "Houston, we have an opportunity!"

Once upon a time, our family car was nearing the end of its useful life, and my wife said to me, "We need a New Car." That, of course, is a *position*. Our *interest* was in finding a way to meet the transportation needs of the family. A New Car would do it, but there could be other ways of addressing that need. The transportation situation had changed a lot since we got our Old Car. A new train station had opened near our home, where before there was none. Our daughter had grown up and was able to get around independently, where before we had to drive her. We now had Uber and other ride-sharing options, which did not exist previously. Times had changed, and we had to change with the times. So I proposed to give my wife and daughter a monthly Transportation Allowance that would allow all of us to get around for much less than the expense of a car, insurance, gas, parking, tolls, road tax, etc. We could save money and fully satisfy our interests, all because I was able to frame the situation in such a way that the alternative to Old Car was Transportation Allowance rather than New Car. It was sheer brilliance!

My wife did not accept my frame, and viewed having a car as non-negotiable. So we ended up getting the New Car. In negotiation as in life, you have to know when to concede.

MAKE IT EASY FOR THEM TO SAY YES

Abraham Lincoln said, "When I'm getting ready to reason with a man, I spend one-third of my time thinking about myself and what I am going to say, and two-thirds thinking about him and what he is going to say." How many negotiators put that much effort into thinking about the other side?

When my daughter first started to walk, she would explore everything within reach. If I went into the storage room, she would follow me and pick up screwdrivers, light bulbs, batteries, and other items not meant for toddlers. I would tell her to put those things down, they were not toys, they were dangerous, she could hurt herself, and so on. None of these reasons worked. I should have known they were doomed to fail, because from her perspective, she had no reason to agree to my demands. She was having fun, and I was asking her to stop having fun. She had nothing to gain and everything to lose.

I had to reformulate my request to make it acceptable to her. I asked her, "Would you like to close the door?" I can only imagine her thought process: "*Close the door? I've never done that before, but I think I can do it. It sounds like fun. My dad will be so proud of me.*" She immediately dropped everything, slammed the door shut, and ran off with a triumphant grin on her face. She gave me exactly what I wanted, but I had to present it to her in a way that appealed to her interests. She viewed this as a net gain for her, and so agreed to my request. There was nothing to negotiate or clarify, she could simply say yes.

I like to think I am more powerful than my daughter and can demand her compliance. By traditional measures of power such as size and strength, I am more powerful than she is. A lot of negotiators like to think this way. However, it is counterproductive. It causes resentment and harms the relationship. Wouldn't it be better to gain someone's willing and enthusiastic cooperation rather than her grudging compliance?

The key to reaching an agreement or resolving a conflict lies in understanding the way the other person sees things. While it is certainly important to think about what we really want and how to get it, we need to think even more about our counterpart, what he wants, and why he might agree to our request.

You are not simply making a request. You are asking the other person to make a decision—to accept your proposal or reject it. Ask yourself these questions:

- What do I want him to do? Is my request clear?
- From his perspective, why would he agree to do it?
- How will he view the consequences of doing or not doing what I ask?

This exercise should give you some new insights. Your demand must be realistic—something your counterpart could agree to. You may conclude: *There's no way he will ever agree to that!* If that is your first reaction, it will probably be your counterpart's as well. So don't ask. Put yourself in the other party's shoes. She won't do anything simply because you want her to do it. She will only do things because she wants to do it. Try to understand what she wants, bearing in mind that she may not want the same things you want. Try to formulate your request so that it makes sense for your counterpart to agree.

One way to do this is by using what Roger Fisher calls a "yesable" proposition.[*] There are two steps to this method. First, put your request into a form where the other party can reply with a clear yes or no. We are not always clear about what we want the other person to do. If our thinking is not clear, our request will not be clear either. If our request is not clear, the other party will not have a clear choice. A confused mind always says no. Cast your request in a form that is so clear and simple that your counterpart's choices could be to check a box marked yes or no.

Second, arrange the incentives and disincentives such that your counterpart finds it advantageous to say yes. No one is likely to agree to anything that does not leave him better off.

Give your counterpart a yesable proposition, a request phrased so she can respond immediately with either a yes or a no. If you truly understand her thinking and interests, and phrase your proposal the right way, you'll get a yes.

---

[*] I first encountered the yesable proposition in Professor Roger Fisher's book *International Conflict for Beginners* (1969). In Fisher's metaphor, it is not enough to let them know there are carrots in the barn (step two); you must first show them the barn door (step one).

ATTITUDE AND CONFIDENCE

The most important tool a win-win negotiator has is his attitude. A win-win negotiator is positive, optimistic, collaborative, and objective. He understands that a win-win outcome is rarely an accident, but the result of systematic application of certain principles. These principles are:

- Approach the negotiation as a problem to be resolved in collaboration with your counterpart. Do not enter a negotiation looking for ways to beat your adversary. Think win-win instead of win-lose. Look for ways to enlarge the pie so that everyone gets a bigger piece.

- Be objective. Don't fall in love with the subject of the negotiation. Be aware of the roles of emotion and biases. Take calculated risks.

- Be positive and optimistic. Aim high. Negotiators with higher aspirations generally end up with more. Set an aggressive anchor and justify it.

- Be persistent. Continue generating options and looking for ways to create value. Remember that the reason win-win outcomes are so rare is not that it can't be done, but that the win-win solution has not been found yet. Compromise only as a last resort.

- Keep your Plan B in mind and be prepared to exercise it. Negotiation is a voluntary process. Be prepared to walk away if you can't get what you want on satisfactory terms. No deal is better than a bad deal.

- Treat the negotiation as a game. Learn the rules and practice the skills. Take the game seriously but not personally. Have fun and try to improve over time.

The most successful negotiators are also confident. Confidence is largely a matter of attitude. You feel ready, positive, and have high expectations. Confidence is also a function of preparation. When you are well prepared you are confident, and when you are not prepared you are not. If you are not prepared, you should not be negotiating.

Confidence is more than just a feeling or state of mind, something internal to you. It is also what the other party sees in you. It is largely a matter of perception. You can appear confident even when you may feel some uncertainty or doubt. You can project confidence by:

- Being comfortable with others and the situation (smile, be friendly and outgoing, calm and relaxed).
- Having strong body language (eye contact, handshake, posture, gestures).
- Speaking in a strong (not necessarily loud), sure, and measured voice. Being articulate and having a deep, low-pitched voice is a big plus.
- Being decisive and avoiding weak words such as maybe, kind of, I guess, um, and so on.
- Looking like a successful businessperson (clothing, grooming, accessories).
- Being enthusiastic!

In business dealings, the more confident person usually prevails. Be that person.

CONSIDER AND EXPLAIN

Most negotiators reject an offer or proposal without giving it much thought. Perhaps they respond immediately with their own counter-offer. They feel they are projecting confidence and strength by showing their conviction about what they want and don't want. They fear that any wavering on their part will be seen as a sign of weakness by the other party. And rejecting a proposal allows them to feel in control: they are in the driver's seat and won't be led around by anyone.

Win-win negotiators know better. An immediate rejection is insulting. It shows a lack of respect. That offer is a product— and an extension—of the other party. You do not help your case by abruptly rejecting your counterpart. By pausing to consider an offer, you show you are taking both the offer and the other person seriously.

Also, by thinking about your counterpart's offer, you just might find some merit in it. You may find some common ground that you would otherwise miss with an out-of-hand rejection. After considering the offer, explain what you like about it and what you don't like. Finding even a shred of value in his offer and working with it will place you in higher regard with your counterpart than if you had rejected his offer completely. Remember, win-win solutions depend on collaboration and joint problem solving, not on prevailing in a battle of wills.

By rejecting an offer, you are saying "I don't like your idea; I want to do it my way." But by considering their offer, focusing on an element that you agree with, and building on it, you can still end up in a place that's acceptable to you—but they think it was their idea! This is the essence of the old saying that diplomacy (which is really negotiation) is the art of letting the other guy have your way.

Finally, give a reason why you don't like the offer. People like to know why. It makes your rejection easier to accept. It also helps your counterpart understand your needs and interests, improving the likelihood of a win-win solution.

KEYS TO A WIN-WIN

While we hear much talk about the coveted win-win outcome, the fact is this result is not common. There are several factors which make a win-win outcome more likely:[*]

- **Focus on interests rather than positions**
  A position is what you say (and perhaps really believe) you want, while an interest is what you truly need from the negotiation. It is not always easy to identify our own true interests, let alone our counterpart's. What we think we want may not be what we really need. Sometimes, we have to think out of the box to see the difference. And you may also learn that your counterpart has no idea what his interests are. Identifying interests—yours and theirs—and addressing those, rather than positions, is a key to negotiating win-win agreements.

---

[*]   Roger Fisher and William Ury, *Getting to Yes* (1981).

- **Know the currencies**

  A currency is anything of value, tangible (money, goods) or intangible (ego, peace of mind, branding), that can be exchanged in a negotiation. Currencies are sometimes hard to identify. If we do not value a certain asset that we possess, we may not realize that our counterpart finds value in it. We may not even be aware that it exists. Understanding the currencies that are available helps us create win-win outcomes.

- **Negotiate multiple issues and create multiple options**

  An option is a possible solution to your negotiation problem. An option is also a package of currencies. There may be many potential solutions to a negotiation. We may only think of one. Or we may think of a few, decide one is the best, and not realize that there may be even better ones out there. The more options we can generate, the more likely we will find one that presents a win-win solution. But if you are negotiating a single issue, such as price, you are setting yourself up for a win-lose or partial win outcome.

- **Use fair and objective standards**

  You need to convince your counterpart (and help her convince her stakeholders) that your proposal has merit. Having a sound standard to measure your proposal against can help you persuade her of the merits. This standard could be a competitive price, precedent, index, industry practice, or some other benchmark.

- **Good communication and sharing information**

  Negotiation is a form of persuasive communication. Most negotiators are reluctant to share information for fear of giving the other party an advantage. This makes it harder for them to help you solve your problem. While some information should not be divulged, sharing information about interests is a key to a win-win.

- **Good relationship based on credibility and trust**

  In business relationships, trust is important in fostering communication and streamlining the negotiation process. A poor relationship or lack of trust is not insurmountable, but it makes negotiating much more challenging.

- **Creative thinking**

  The essence of creativity is making connections between things or ideas, and understanding how they relate to one another. Creative negotiators recognize patterns and know when to follow them and when to break them. Precedents, accepted practices, norms, and other patterns provide us with shortcuts. We follow the pattern and it makes our life easier. At least it does most of the time. However, if you do the things other people do (follow the pattern), you will get the results other people get. If you want something better—such as a win-win—you need to do things differently. Average negotiators come up with obvious solutions. Win-win negotiators think creatively.

We have just glossed over some key concepts in negotiation: positions, interests, currencies, and options. We will discuss them in detail in the next chapter.

CHAPTER 3

POSITIONS, INTERESTS, CURRENCIES, AND OPTIONS

"Price is what you pay. Value is what you get."
— Warren Buffett

POSITIONS VERSUS INTERESTS

One of the keys to reaching a win-win agreement is to understand the difference between *positions* and *interests*. Although the terms are often used interchangeably, they are not the same.

Positions are the demands and offers made by the parties in a negotiation.

Interests are what the parties consider most important to them—what they truly need, or *why* they want it.

Simply stated, a position is what you say you want, while an interest is what would actually satisfy your needs. Believe it or not, many people think they know what they want, yet they may not be aware of what their real interests are.

It may help you to think of interests and positions as parts of an iceberg. Positions are the tip of the iceberg that you can see, while interests are the more substantial part hidden beneath the surface, out of sight and unrecognized. You need to look beneath the surface to uncover what's really important.

For example, suppose you ask your boss for a raise. Your boss tells you that he would like to grant your request but there is no money in the budget for a raise. You then either quit your job for one that pays better and hope you like it as much as your previous job, or you continue to work unhappily while the resentment builds. Nobody wins.

Do you really need a raise? Or is that simply your position, that is, what you think you want? Why do you want a raise? What is your real interest? It's probably not the money itself, but some means of maintaining or improving your lifestyle. While a raise could help you satisfy this interest, there are also other ways to satisfy it. A company car, health benefits, or a housing allowance might serve the purpose as well. Your boss might be able to satisfy your interests through one of these means, even if a raise is out of the question.

A position may be a means to satisfy an interest, but it is not necessarily the only way—or the best way—to do so.

Focusing on positions is not productive. It often leads to interests being overlooked. If you advance your position of wanting a raise, your boss will defend his position of being unable to give you one, and neither of you would consider other options that might address your interests.

People become attached to their positions. If they abandon or change a position, they appear wishy-washy and lose face. Defending your position can be against your interests, yet you may not notice it as you strive to project strength and consistency. This can get personal and damage the relationship between the parties.

Don't get bogged down in positions. Instead, focus on your interests, what is most important to you. It's also important that you can satisfy the interests of the other party, at least in part, or they may not continue to negotiate with you.

IDENTIFYING INTERESTS

For each position advanced by you or your counterpart, you need to ask: "Why? What purpose does it serve?" This enables you to uncover the underlying interest behind each position. A rule of thumb is to determine whether there is more than one way to satisfy a demand. If not, you are dealing with an interest.

For example, you may want a pay raise as a form of recognition by your company of your value and contribution over the years. There may be other ways of getting the recognition you crave: a new title, a promotion, more perks, or additional responsibilities. Thus your opening position might be "I want a raise," but your true interest might be "I deserve more recognition."

You may have heard an old story about two sisters squabbling over an orange. Each sister clings to her own position, which is that *she* is entitled to the orange. Obviously, they cannot *both* have the orange. Eventually, after much argument, the sisters reveal their true interests. One wants orange juice, and the other wants to grate the rind to flavor a cake.

The sisters' original positions are incompatible and mutually exclusive. If one gets the orange, the other doesn't—a win-lose outcome. Or they can do what most fair-minded people will do: compromise! They could cut the orange in half, so each gets something but neither gets what she wants. Perhaps half an orange does not yield enough juice to satisfy one sister's thirst, and does not have enough rind to flavor a cake. In addition, some of the juice and rind are unproductively given to the party who does not value it. Ideally, you want to optimize the allocation of all the currencies available in a negotiation, without any leakage.

Only by identifying and sharing their interests do they find a way for each sister to get everything she wants. In this way, both parties may be able to satisfy their interests fully, even when their positions are incompatible.

You may think that the story of the squabbling sisters is quaint and contrived, and that nothing like it could ever happen in the real world. It can and it does, and for very high stakes.

In 1979, Egypt and Israel signed a peace treaty. A major stumbling block to the agreement had been the disposition of the Sinai Peninsula. Historically part of Egypt, it was captured by Israel during the Six Day War in 1967. Israel insisted on retaining all or part of it, while Egypt demanded the entire area. The positions were clearly incompatible.

Agreement was reached only after both parties' interests were addressed. Israel did not really want the land per se; it wanted the security buffer the land provided. Egypt did not require all of the attributes of sovereignty; it only wanted its traditional patrimony to be made whole. It was willing to demilitarize portions of it to achieve its main interest. Israel returned the land in exchange for security guarantees, and both parties' interests were satisfied in full—a win-win outcome.

PRIORITIZING INTERESTS

Make a wish list of all the things you could possibly get out of a negotiation. For each item, ask yourself "Why?" (perhaps more than once) to determine your true interests. Prioritize them so you are clear on which are most important to you. For a simple negotiation, it might be enough to create three categories: high, medium, and low priorities, or the three categories may be: what you must have, what you really want, and what would be nice to have.

It is tempting to say, "Everything is important to me! I want this and this and that!" But not everything is equally important. To be more realistic and disciplined about your priorities, list all of your interests. Then assign each interest a numerical weight such that the weighted value of all your interests totals 100 points. This will help you focus your attention on what matters to you most. It will protect you from exchanging good value for something trivial (a shiny bauble!) while forgetting all about your main objectives.

Try to anticipate the other party's interests and priorities as well. You may not be able to rank them with precision, but you could probably determine which ones he considers to be very important, somewhat important, or of low importance.

SHARING INFORMATION ABOUT INTERESTS

It's amazing how secretive people can be during a negotiation. Negotiators talk and listen to one another, but they often do not share much information. No doubt this is because information is power, and we want to have more power than the other party. We behave as though anything we say will be used against us. However, hoarding information and treating every bit of data like it's top secret is counterproductive.

Most negotiators are far more guarded about disclosing information than they should be. Recall that negotiation can be thought of as joint problem solving. If you don't share information with your counterpart, how can she help you solve your problem? If your counterpart knows your interests, she might be able to think of a solution that you may have overlooked. As the old saying goes, two heads are better than one.

Remember our squabbling sisters? In the heat of conflict, they see each other as rivals and may not be inclined to communicate freely, much less share critical information. But what if one had said "I need the orange because I want to grate the rind for my cake"? Chances are the other would have replied "Is that all? I only want a glass of orange juice." Problem solved.

Sharing information about interests increases the likelihood of a win-win outcome. It also encourages trust. After all, it's hard to trust someone who acts secretively. If you share information, your counterpart is likely to reciprocate. You both benefit.

But what if they don't reciprocate? Will that put you at a disadvantage? The answer is no. Sharing information about interests is a key to a win-win result, *even if the other party does not reciprocate*. By making your interests known, they are more likely to be able to help you. You need not agree to anything that does not satisfy your interests, and knowledge of your interests by the other party can help her find a way to satisfy them. If you share information about your interests and they don't reciprocate, it only makes it harder for you to help *them*.

The general rule is that you should share information about your interests. Think carefully about whether to share other kinds of information. You may not want to share information about your bottom line, your Plan B, deadlines, trade secrets, or other sensitive matters, at least not right away. But don't assume that sensitive information should never be revealed. Reassess the value of sharing sensitive information as the negotiation progresses.

For example, you probably would not volunteer information about your budget or time constraints early on. If a salesman knew what your budget was, he would find a way to get all of it. But let's say you were willing to spend your entire budget, but the salesman kept demanding more. Revealing your budget would provide a reality check, and once he realized he couldn't get his demand, he might become more accommodating in order to close the deal.

Similarly, suppose you had a tight deadline. If your counterpart knew you were on a tight deadline, he might use that to pressure you into a deal that was not very favorable for you. But if you were happy with your proposal and your counterpart was using delay tactics to try to get more from you, you might reveal your deadline and pressure him to accept your terms quickly.

As the negotiation unfolds, information that could hurt you if revealed too soon might later be used to your advantage. Continuously reassess whether a certain piece of information is best shared or kept secret.

CURRENCIES

A currency is *anything* of value—tangible or intangible—that can be exchanged in a negotiation. Of course, the best known currency is money. There is also the product or service the money is being exchanged for. But there are many other currencies, including method of payment, delivery schedule, allocation of risk, timing, other terms and conditions, brand and reputation, emotional needs, perceptions, and anything else of value. It isn't just about price.

If you *are* negotiating only on price, you are setting yourself up for a win-lose outcome. For example, let's say we are negotiating the price of bottled water. Every extra dollar in my pocket is one less dollar for you. But if I buy a thousand cases, can I get a discount? And what if I pay cash today rather than send you a check in thirty days? And what if I want the name of my business printed on the label? Or a fancy, faux crystal bottle design instead of the plain one? Now we have a lot of currencies we can trade, not just price. The more currencies we can introduce into the mix, the more options we have, and the better the chances that one of them will be a win-win.

How do you prepare for exchanging currencies in a negotiation? First, make a list of everything you have that your counterpart might want as part of a deal. I mean everything. Your counterpart may have many needs that are not readily apparent, including emotional and intangible ones. For example, a salesperson may be less interested in a high price or commission than getting a quick sale that will impress her boss, winning the monthly sales contest, or boosting her sagging morale. The more of these needs you can identify and offer to meet, the more value you have.

Then think of everything your counterpart has that you might want as part of an agreement. You probably won't get everything on the list, but the point is to be aware of what's out there. Then prioritize this list as discussed earlier. This will help you focus on your true interests and not get distracted by baubles.

I often ask the participants in my negotiation seminars whether they would like to negotiate with Donald Trump. Most smile nervously as they say no. "Why not?" I ask, although I already know the answer. They do not believe they would fare well in a negotiation with the tough, intimidating, and business-savvy Trump.

A few, however, raise their hand to indicate that they would like to do a deal with The Donald. Their reasoning is usually that they may not make the best deal, but they would learn from the experience.

I suggest there is another reason: it would be a great story to tell future negotiating partners. Imagine … You're in the middle of a negotiation, and you say, "This reminds me of a deal we made with Donald Trump a few months ago. We agreed to blah blah blah blah blah …" Your negotiating partner is now thinking, "*Wow! This guy did a deal with Donald Trump? I'm impressed—he must really be a bigger bigwig than I thought! I've got to close this deal.*" It would be great for your reputation—and your ego—to be able to drop Trump's name in this manner. And you can be sure Donald Trump knows that dealing with him is a currency that has intangible yet very real value, and factors it into his negotiating demands!

You may not be a celebrity like Donald Trump, but you might be able to identify other hard to recognize currencies and extract added value from them.

Many years ago I attended a Cheap Trick concert. Rick Nielsen, the lead guitarist, had a habit of flinging his picks into the audience and quickly grabbing another one to continue playing. All night long the picks were flying around me, but I didn't get one. This was before the Internet or eBay, so if I was to get a pick, I had to get it then and there.

After the final encore I walked up to the stage, hoping to find one. No luck. I called out to one of the roadies, who was busy packing up equipment.

"Hey, are there any more picks?"

"Sorry dude, they're all gone. *Cough, cough … hack … cough, cough!*"

"It sounds like you've got a bad cough."

"Yeah man, my throat's killing me. *Cough, cough.*"

It was winter and we were outdoors. I also had a cough. And I had a pocketful of cough drops. I saw my opportunity.

"I've got some cough drops. If you can find me a pick, they're yours."

He went into the band's trailer and came out a few minutes later with a pick. We made the trade. Win-win!

I got a piece of genuine rock and roll memorabilia worthy of a spot in the Hard Rock Cafe, something I valued highly. What did I give up for it? A handful of cough drops. Cost to me: zero. I had a whole bag of them at home, twenty minutes away.

The roadie, with a few hours of work in the cold night air ahead of him, without a car in a strange city, and with no drugstore nearby, got the one thing that could make his life better at that moment. And what did it cost him to give me the pick? Nothing! He nicked it from the guitar player!

We each got something we valued highly without giving up anything of value to us. This is negotiating alchemy, creating value out of nothing. Sweet!

Was it just luck? No. I understood my counterpart's needs. I was also aware of the currencies, even though he did not know I had cough drops. Often, one or both parties is not aware of the currencies. That's the value of information exchange.

While I was delighted with the result, I later realized that I might have done better. I should have asked for the guitar!

THE ALCHEMY OF NEGOTIATION: LEVERAGING CURRENCIES

It is easy to assume that others see things as we do. After all, we are rational, successful, and must have done something right to end up where we are today. Surely we know what is right, good, and important. If we want something, everyone else must want it too. If we value something, others must value it as well.

Of course, we all see things differently. One sister sees an orange and wants juice, another sees it and wants to bake a cake. One values the juice and has no use for the rind, but the other needs the rind and doesn't care about the juice.

One country wants land, and another only wants security.

One employee wants recognition, and another only wants more money.

We all have our own ideas about what we want, and that's a good thing. It gives us a better chance of finding a win-win solution.

The problem is our mistaken assumption that others are like us. We need to learn that others are different and recognize—and exploit—these differences. The fact that others may value things differently creates an opportunity for a win-win outcome.

Somewhere in the wilderness, a cow defecates. This waste product, as the term implies, has no value to the cow. A farmer stumbles upon the dung. He thinks to himself, "*I can use this dung to make bricks and build a house. I can use this as fuel to cook my dinner and warm my family. I can use this to fertilize my crops and improve my livelihood.*" To the farmer, this waste product is like gold.

Closer to home, a restaurant manager ponders what to do with her used cooking oil. She could dump it in the alley, creating a stench and risking a citation from the health inspector. She could pay a waste removal company to dispose of it. Or, she could sell it to a company that converts used oil into fuel.

One man's trash is another man's treasure. At times you will find that you value something far more than the other party, and vice versa. This is an ideal opportunity to create value. If you can give the other side something it values highly at little or no cost to yourself, you can get a lot of mileage out of it. Perhaps they can do the same for you. Now you each give up a little to gain a lot. You are creating value out of nothing (or almost nothing)! This is a key to reaching win-win agreements.

Kyle MacDonald was a Canadian handyman, blogger, and aspiring writer. In 2005, he went online and offered to trade a red paper clip for anything of greater value. About one year later, he completed his 14th and final trade, each time leveraging greater value. His trades were:

- a red paper clip
- a novelty pen shaped like a fish
- a handmade ceramic doorknob
- a camping stove
- a 1,000-watt generator
- a beer keg with neon Budweiser sign
- a snowmobile
- a trip to Yahk in the Canadian Rockies
- a van
- a recording contract
- one year of rent-free accommodation in a house in Phoenix, Arizona

- an afternoon hanging out with rock star Alice Cooper
- a Kiss (the rock band, not the candy) snow globe
- a paid speaking role in a Hollywood movie
- a two-story farmhouse in Kipling, Saskatchewan, Canada

Several of MacDonald's trades appear to be for items of comparable value. For example, trading a generator for a beer keg and neon sign sounds equitable.

Some of his transactions, however, appear ludicrous, for example, a snow globe for a movie role. Most people would value a snow globe at only a few dollars, if they wanted it at all. But if you have a huge collection of snow globes, you might be willing to pay a high price for a special acquisition. And while many people would kill for a movie role, a Hollywood producer has plenty of them, and filling them can be a chore.

These differences in the way individuals assign value to currencies open up a world of possibilities and increase the likelihood of a favorable result in a negotiation.

Some of MacDonald's traders valued more than the tangible items they were exchanging. They may have valued being part of this wacky quest, getting a small measure of fame, or perhaps they just wanted to help.

The town of Kipling gave up a house, but got a lot in return. They held American Idol-style auditions to fill the movie role, raised some money for the town coffers, and put up the world's largest red paper clip as a town landmark, all generating a huge amount of publicity (by Kipling standards). These currencies—though hard to value in dollars—were important to the town.

Kyle MacDonald got much more than a house for his efforts. He published a book chronicling his experience and launched a speaking career. He's doing well enough that he donated the house back to the town of Kipling. And he got to meet Alice Cooper anyway.

To identify items that may be valued differently by the parties, here are some things to consider:

- **Perceptions**
Some people will pay more to save face, look good, or have their ego stroked. They will pay a high price for a shirt with a designer's logo stitched onto it, even though a similar shirt—same style, color, and fabric—may be available without any logo for much less. Some people will only wear a shirt with a particular logo, some are indifferent as to the logo, and still others hate the idea of advertising for a designer and would rather have a plain shirt. The perception of value is important, though it varies among individuals.

- **Risk**

  People have different risk profiles. Some people are risk averse, while others boldly accept risk. A more risk averse party may be willing to concede more if her negotiating counterpart is willing to assume certain risks involved in the transaction. Most people hate risk and buy insurance to mitigate it, while insurance companies love risk because it's very profitable for them.

- **Combining similar resources and skills to achieve economies of scale**

  There is power in size, and there is power in numbers. Two or more parties can pool their demands to negotiate more favorable rates from suppliers. For example, a small neighborhood supermarket does not have the negotiating power of Walmart, but a number of independent grocers can band together to negotiate lower prices from a food producer.

- **Combining different resources and skills to accomplish together what neither can do alone**

  Entities with complementary attributes can create synergy. For example, a landowner and a building contractor can form a joint venture to develop the property and get a better return than either might have otherwise enjoyed.

By exchanging currencies that are valued differently, each side can get more by giving up less! What painless concessions can you make that might be valued by the other party? What might they easily do for you that would be of great value to you? By focusing on interests and exploiting differently valued currencies, you are more likely to attain a win-win outcome.

OPTIONS

The purpose of negotiation is not just to convince the other side to let us have what we want. It is to improve our situation such that each of us is better off than we would have been absent an agreement. It is to solve a problem jointly for mutual benefit, rather than to compete for gain at the other's expense. The solution to the negotiation puzzle—whether we are better off than we would have been without negotiating—is a function of the choices available to us, that is, our options.

An option is a possible solution to a negotiation. Looked at another way, an option is a package of currencies. The more options we can create, the greater the likelihood that one will be a win-win solution.

Returning to the case of the two sisters and the orange, what were their options? How could they have solved their problem? Sister A could have let Sister B have the orange, or Sister B could have let Sister A have it. They could have cut the orange in half in a misguided attempt at compromise. They could have tossed a coin or drawn lots to decide ownership. They could have fought over it. They could have bid for it. They could have brought in other currencies (a banana, strawberries, choice of which program to watch on TV) and agreed on some distribution of all the fruit (and control of the remote). Ultimately, they found the one option out of many that gave them a win-win result: one squeezed out the juice and the other grated the rind.

The sisters had quite a few options, and there are no doubt others we haven't considered. Most of them were win-lose or partial win solutions. Only one was a win-win. Most of the options, although unsatisfactory, were easy to conceive. The win-win was more challenging. Too often, a negotiator will accept an outcome he deems good enough because it is easy. A great negotiator understands how to identify currencies, combine them into options, and design an option that maximizes and optimizes.

OUR THREE FAVORITE OPTIONS

Most negotiators begin with three options in mind:

1. The best deal I can get (usually a hard to attain ideal).
2. The worst deal I will accept (just better than the walk away point).
3. The most likely agreement I believe we can reach (which usually involves an inefficient compromise).

There are several problems with this limited range of options. First of all, you don't really know the best deal you can get. You may have certain expectations based on your assumptions about what your counterpart has and wants, and within the context of your necessarily limited world view. There might be something better for you and you might not even see it because you are locked into your original position.

Similarly, you can't be sure of the worst deal you will accept. You may have a bottom line price in mind, but the introduction of other currencies or new information could influence you to change that. For example, you may decide that the lowest price you will accept for your widgets is 93 cents per unit, but you may be willing to accept less if the buyer pays cash, or takes delivery at your factory, or orders an unusually large volume, or if he also buys some monogrammed widget covers, etc.

Furthermore, having this limited range of options in mind may give you false confidence that you are prepared, and it is essential to prepare for a negotiation in the face of uncertainty. However, this is not the way to do it. It would set a range based on arbitrary positions rather than interests.

Start generating options by listing and prioritizing your interests, then listing all of your currencies. List your counterpart's interests and currencies as best you can. Remember, options are possible solutions to your negotiation. Currencies are the building blocks of options.

CREATING OPTIONS FROM CURRENCIES

To prepare well for a negotiation, you must first understand what you really want. You would be surprised to find that many people are not even sure of what they want.

Next, try to anticipate what your counterpart wants. You may never be sure of what he wants, but with a little foresight and research you can get a pretty good idea. Remember to test your assumptions later during your discussions—while laying the foundation and bargaining.

Finally, combine these currencies into a range of packages, or options. The more interests and options you have on the table, the greater the chance of a win-win agreement.

By focusing on options that promote interests rather than positions, we can create more value for each side. Each party may offer certain currencies to entice the other party. Recall that an option is one of a range of possible packages of currencies, for example:

Option 1   Party A offers currencies A, B, C
           Party B offers currencies X, Y, Z
Option 2   Party A offers currencies A, D, F
           Party B offers currencies V, Y, Z
Option 3   Party A offers currencies A, D, E
           Party B offers currencies W, X, Y, Z

And so on.

Any option (set of currencies) is a potential solution. Obviously, you would prefer to offer the smallest, cheapest, and easiest currencies that would be acceptable to the other party. Bear in mind that what's cheap and easy for you may be highly valued by them.

MULTIPLE EQUIVALENT SIMULTANEOUS OFFERS (MESOs)

One way to gain insight into what your counterpart values most is by pure trial and error. After making offers and counter-offers and getting rejections, you try to figure out what she wants or doesn't want. This is time-consuming and inefficient, and may not provide much insight into what she is looking for.

A better way is to use MESOs. You can ask your counterpart "Do you prefer Option 1 or 2?" Recall that an option is a package of currencies, and you can create many options by arranging different currencies into packages. If she prefers neither, ask her what she likes or doesn't like about those options. Based on that information, offer her Options 2 and 3. Continue until you have an agreement.

Here's an analogy for how to use MESOs. When you're having your eyeglass prescription checked the optometrist doesn't just give you a box of glasses and let you try them on at random until you find the best one. That would be pointless. Instead, he takes a systematic approach. He will put the big goggles on you and switch lenses and ask "Is this better ... [switch] ... or this? This one ... [switch] ... or this?" You quickly zero in on the right lens and you're done! That's pretty much how the MESO concept works.

The big letter on top of the optometrist's chart is the "E". That's also important in MESO. The Multiple Offers you are Simultaneously presenting to your counterpart should be Equivalent to you. In other words, you are equally willing to go with Option 1 or 2, but you are trying to calibrate what works better for your counterpart.

Using MESOs signals to your counterpart that you are flexible and interested in their preferences. You're not just forcing your proposal on them. It also allows you to gather information about their interests, enabling you to match options to their needs and systematically improve the chances of reaching a win-win agreement.

CHAPTER 4

NEGOTIATING POWER AND YOUR PLAN B

"You got to know when to hold 'em, know when to fold 'em, know when to walk away and know when to run."
— Kenny Rogers, "The Gambler"

I often ask the participants in my negotiation seminars this question: who has more negotiating power in one of their typical negotiations, them or their counterpart? The vast majority believe their counterpart has more power. This doesn't make much sense mathematically—we would expect the number to average about 50%. You can infer two things from this:

1. it is very common for a negotiator to feel that the other party has the upper hand; and
2. if so many people feel that the other party has more power than they do, there's a very good chance that your counterpart believes you have an advantage over him!

Perhaps you also feel powerless compared to the people you negotiate with. Take heart from the finding above, and be aware that there are many kinds of negotiating power. If you are lacking in some, you may be able to compensate with some of the other types of power.

LEGITIMATE POWER

Legitimate power refers to power associated with a position or office. For example, a vice president of a major corporation or the head of a government department has the power that comes with the position. Whoever holds the office holds the power, regardless of their intellect, competence, or personality.

Legitimate power often manifests itself through an impressive title, a magnificent office desk and chair, and a luxuriously appointed conference room. The holder of such power has influence with political bigwigs and corporate titans, instant access to the media, and an army of lackeys to do his bidding. He wears expensive tailored suits, sports a fine Swiss watch, and entertains clients at the most exclusive clubs. It is easy to see how anyone not part of his exalted circle could feel intimidated.

You may not have a fancy title like your negotiating partner, but some titles are just a lot of hot air. Despite your counterpart's senior title, power suit, and club membership, you may be dealing with a weak negotiator.

You will be painfully aware of your own deadlines, sales targets, budget constraints, and other pressure points. However, you probably don't know what pressures your counterpart is under, and it is unlikely that he will tell you. Everyone has problems, worries, and weaknesses, even Donald Trump and Sir Richard Branson.

Most people tend to overestimate their own pressures and weaknesses, while assuming their counterpart has a stronger position. When you face a seemingly powerful negotiating partner, it's a good idea to remind yourself that she may have problems of her own. Perhaps she is under pressure to conclude a deal with you, and may not have as strong a hand as she is leading you to believe. You must ignore the trappings of power and focus on your interests.

Bear in mind also that traditional sources of power such as money and position are less important than they used to be, relative to other types of power.

EXPERTISE

An expert is a person who possesses extraordinary skill or knowledge in a particular area. In today's complex, highly specialized world, expertise is a more important source of power than a title.

For example, I've had teenagers help me with computer problems. Despite their youth and lack of a title, these youngsters have power over me due to their superior expertise in the field of computers. When they tell me I need a new thingamabob, I get it. When they say it costs x dollars, I pay it.

Expertise is perhaps the most important form of power today, and anyone can develop it. What type of expertise do you have? How can you develop more expertise in that area, or in complementary areas? By increasing your expertise, you increase your negotiating power.

Perhaps your expertise is well-known. If not, you must let the other party know (subtly, of course) that you are an expert. Make sure he is aware of your credentials. Ask questions that show a high level of understanding, use the appropriate jargon, and refer to other experiences where relevant. You may be able to influence the other party and achieve a more favorable outcome if he recognizes your expertise.

Projecting expertise is subject to posturing and hype. It would pay to remember this when you find yourself negotiating with a so-called expert. Do not be taken in by the title, smooth talk, or cocky demeanor. It could all be an act. In any case, he is only human, and you both stand to gain from the negotiation.

If you are truly dealing with a bona fide expert, do not be intimidated. Experts are not always right, and their opinion is often just that—an opinion. In almost any major lawsuit, each party will engage an expert. These experts will contradict each other on every critical point. They cannot both be right! Don't assume the expert opposite you is right either.

INFORMATION
Information is another source of negotiating power. The more you know about your counterpart, the subject of the negotiation, and your respective industries, the more power you have. For example:

- What does your counterpart really need? What are his true interests? What are his psychological and ego needs?
- Who are his constituents or stakeholders? What are their interests?

- Who are his competitors? What competitive pressures is he facing?
- What is his negotiating style? What tactics does he use?
- What is his financial situation? What are his budget constraints?
- Does he have any deadlines or time constraints? What is his business cycle like?
- Are there any relevant trends or changes happening in his industry?
- Is there anything in his background or track record of interest to you?

It is easier to gather information before you begin bargaining. Once you begin talking with your counterpart, you may find him reluctant to disclose much information, and he may be suspicious of your motives. Begin gathering information as soon as you realize you have an interest that you will have to negotiate to satisfy.

Let's say you want to buy a new computer. Most people would simply go to a dealer, look at a few models, and buy one they think would be suitable. They may later find that it does not meet their needs or that they paid too much for it.

A good negotiator would first determine exactly what her needs are. Then she would research various models that could meet those needs. She would then compare prices at different dealers for her top two or three choices. A really good negotiator would even research the dealers to learn about their business practices and negotiating styles.

It is particularly useful to get information about the other party's needs and interests. Understanding the other party and his interests can give you a tremendous advantage. Find out everything you can about your counterpart, his company, and his needs.

Note that people have many needs, and not all of them are obvious. Do not overlook psychological or ego needs, which we will discuss in Chapter 6.

You can find a lot of valuable information online, in industry directories, and in trade journals. Annual reports and other company publications are also full of useful information. You might also talk to people who have previously dealt with the person or organization you will be negotiating with, or read reviews online. With all the information available on the Internet today, it is easier than ever to boost your negotiating power.

You can even talk to other people within your counterpart's organization. When shopping for that new computer, wouldn't it be useful to speak candidly with a service technician *before* you approach a salesman? Wouldn't the technician give you valuable information about the pros and cons of various models, even competitors' models, that the salesman would not mention while he is selling to you? That technician would be so flattered that you asked for his opinion that he would lay it all out for you!

Information is like gold. Begin gathering information as early as possible. This is the fastest and easiest way to increase your negotiating power.

I was sailing the Caribbean on a cruise when the "pirate" attacked. "I see you're interested in the Max," said the young lady in the little black dress (or LBD, the unofficial uniform of art gallery saleswomen). "I have a couple of other Maxes," she cooed, leading me deeper into the section of the ship that served as the on-board art gallery. "Do you collect Max?" she purred.

LBD showed me her art, invited me to the upcoming art auction, introduced me to her boss (who could make things happen, she promised), and told me she could give me a special deal if I was serious about any of the Maxes. She even slipped some coupons good for additional discounts under my cabin door that night. She was working hard.

I went to the auction but kept a low profile. There were a lot of big names among the artists represented, but sales were sluggish. LBD seemed to be taking bids out of nowhere. Could this really be the world's largest art gallery? Well, if your business model involves having your inventory on dozens of cruise ships around the world, you might be able to make such a claim. The idea of buying fine art on a cruise ship, however, seemed like a disconnect and there were a number of other nagging doubts in my mind, including the fact that it was not a good idea to bid at an auction unless you had a thorough knowledge of the subject. I did not know much about this art or what a good price would be. So long, Max.

When I got back to dry land (and an Internet connection), I did some research. This gallery with the New York sounding name was actually in the Midwest. It was afflicted with a lot of complaints, legal actions, and just plain bad luck. It also turns out that auctions conducted on the high seas are not subject to the legal niceties of doing business in a land-based jurisdiction. Peter Max, the iconic pop artist, was still alive and creating art. Lots of art. Mostly painting a few details and his signature onto mass-produced works. I saw loads of them on eBay, most at asking prices below those of LBD's.

What can we learn from this voyage?

- Don't succumb to flattery. Don't flatter yourself either, but know yourself.
- Never rush into a major purchase. Do your homework and shop around.
- There are always good deals to be had, but it takes work to find them. They don't scream "GOOD DEAL" in flashing lights, and they don't usually come with coupons.
- When you are isolated at sea without phone or Internet access, you are at a serious disadvantage. You can also negotiate in the dark on land. Negotiate only when you have adequate information.
- Nobody goes on a cruise to buy fine art, so don't buy any on a cruise. You can buy cheap art anywhere, if you like it.
- Beware the LBD—they wear them for a reason.

REWARD AND PUNISHMENT

We negotiate with someone because we believe he is in a position to help us or hurt us. We want him to help us, or to refrain from hurting us, and we negotiate to try to influence that outcome. We are also in a position to help or hurt our counterpart. Therefore, we each have some measure of power to reward or punish the other.

Whether a party will use that power to reward or punish is a matter of perception. So is the more basic question of whether a party even has such power, and how much. If you feel they have power, then they do. And if they feel you have power over them, then you do. Do not wield your power like a club. Let them think you have power, and never disabuse them of that notion, whether it is accurate or not. It is better to keep them guessing than to limit yourself by minimizing their perception of your power.

COMPETITION

Competition is another form of negotiating power. If you have ever bid on a government project, you will know how powerful competition can be. The thought that someone else will offer to do the job for less presses you to lower your bid. Since the number of jobs available is relatively scarce and many bidders are competing for them, the government benefits.

Whenever there is competition for what you are offering—whether it's money, products, services, or time—others will value it more. Remind your counterpart that he has competition, or that you have other alternatives. Never appear too eager for a deal. Always have a Plan B, as discussed below.

RATIONALE

A rationale is an external, objective standard for evaluating possible negotiating outcomes. "Because I said so" is not a rationale, nor is "That's my bottom line" or "Take it or leave it." Your rationale provides an objective standard against which you can measure the reasonableness and fairness of a proposed outcome. Possible standards include market value, custom, precedent, previous course of dealings, expert opinion, cost, efficiency, industry standards, indices or benchmarks, etc.

Having a persuasive rationale is a strong form of negotiating power. It shows you are being fair-minded and objective rather than arbitrary. In addition, a reasonable standard helps you to maintain credibility. It helps your counterpart to sell the result to his boss or other stakeholders. It gives your counterpart a reason to agree with you.

The negotiation must also be perceived as being procedurally fair. Fairness is universally one of the strongest rationales, although there are different ideas about what is fair. If you don't like the rationale advanced by the other party, ask "What makes that fair?" They may be able to persuade you, or they may acknowledge the unfairness and relent. In any event, many negotiators feel better about having a fair process than getting the best outcome substantively.

Of course, a party can advance a number of rationales. Some will be more persuasive than others, and some will be more favorable to you than others. You want to use a rationale that is persuasive to your counterpart and produces an acceptable (if not the best) result for you. Your task is to develop a range of objective standards and prioritize them in order of preference to you. Also, anticipate the rationales your counterpart might advance and which are most favorable to them, and be prepared to dispute them.

For example, suppose you are negotiating the lease amount for office space. You could use a number of possible standards (see below). All of these can be rationally justified. Of course, you would first suggest the option most favorable to you. To do so, arrange the options on a continuum from most to least favorable:

- $12.00 rate paid by previous tenant
- $13.20 rate paid by previous tenant plus an adjustment for inflation
- $14.00 best rate available elsewhere (Plan B)
- $14.50 rate of comparable space in comparable building

Thus, you would first offer $12.00 per square foot, arguing that it is fair to pay the same rate today as the previous tenant paid yesterday. The leasing agent would probably argue that you should pay $14.50 because it is the going rate for comparable space. While any of these options would be justifiable, you would not want to pay more than $14.00 (your Plan B).

Why would the leasing agent accept your $14.00 when the market rate is $14.50, and her boss is also expecting $14.50? You have to provide a rationale: "We're a good tenant, we have a sterling reputation, we pay our rent on time, we bring a lot of valuable foot traffic to your building, every month the space sits empty you're losing money, etc." Will her boss accept the deal? If she can sell him on it, with your help.

If you engage in the same type of negotiation repeatedly (such as office leases), you should use the same rationale for each one. If you pick and choose according to what is most favorable to you in that particular instance, your credibility will suffer. In this case, you want to advance the rationale that is most advantageous to you most of the time and stick with it.

PRECEDENT

A court of law will nearly always follow precedent when handing down a judgment. Precedent refers to the practice of following previous outcomes in similar cases. It allows the courts to be consistent, and it allows citizens to predict whether a proposed course of action is likely to have negative consequences. Society benefits from this fairness and predictability.

In law, precedent is binding. In other fields, we often act as though it were as well. The same rationale applies. We like and accept precedent because it makes our life easier, and we like doing things the way they've been done before. So it's a good idea to appeal to precedent whenever it serves your interests.

What if following precedent goes against your interests in a particular situation? Then argue against it. Differentiate your case from the others, and show how this distinction warrants different treatment.

For example, suppose you are negotiating with your boss for a salary increase. You could use precedent to show how other employees in the same position with the same experience and performance are earning more than you, so your request is justified. Your boss might try to find a reason why the precedent should not be followed. Perhaps a poor economy or some other factor makes your comparison irrelevant.

Precedent is a powerful justification for getting people to do something. Use that power when you can, and be prepared to fight it when you must.

COMMITMENT

As you prepare for a negotiation, get the commitment of others on your team. Ask for their input and involvement. Get their buy-in. Their full support is a source of power.

Commitment is the difference between "Let's give it a try" and "Failure is not an option." Commitment from your team means you are all in this together. All share the risk and reward. Knowing your team is with you gives you confidence. You will feel stronger, and your counterpart will notice this. This psychological edge will help you throughout the negotiation.

The advantage isn't just psychological. Your team's input will help you prepare better because you draw on multiple perspectives and strengths. You will benefit as their knowledge and expertise supplement your own.

INVESTMENT

People don't like to lose. We don't like to lose money, waste time, or invest effort without gain. It follows that the more we invest in a negotiation—time, money, effort, or psychic energy—the more we want to get something in return. This fear of seeing our investment go down the drain may lead us to accept a poor settlement.

The voice of wisdom tells us that it is better to see our investment gone than to make the situation worse by accepting a bad deal. Unfortunately, we don't always heed this voice.

Be mindful of what you and your counterpart invest in a negotiation. Learn to see your investment as sunk costs that are gone regardless of whether you are able to conclude a satisfactory agreement. However, you don't need to educate your counterpart on this point. Let him see his investment as a reason to reach an agreement with you. You might even remind your counterpart of his investment. "It's too bad you can't raise your offer any higher. After all the time we've spent on this, it would be a shame to walk away empty-handed. Are you sure you can't find a bit more money in the budget?"

You can even leverage on your counterpart's investment. Negotiate and agree on the easier issues first. Save the difficult ones for last. In light of his investment, your counterpart may become more accommodating on the tougher issues.

PERSISTENCE

When you were a toddler, you were eager to walk about like everyone else. Imagine if you had quit trying to walk the first time you fell down. You'd still be crawling around on the floor today! But you persisted, because you wanted it badly enough.

Most people give up too easily. They try something, they fail, and they quit. They ask for something, they get a no, and they give up. They are afraid to pursue the matter for fear of failing again. They stop asking in case they are seen as overbearing, or because they don't want to risk further rejection.

The word no is not carved in stone. It is usually a gut reaction to a proposal that has not been well considered. The same request, in another time and place, might get a yes. When you hear a no, treat it as an opening position. Make a counter-offer. Modify your request. Explore other possibilities. Be persistent. You just may succeed in turning that no into a yes.

Every negotiation begins with the word no—if they said yes you wouldn't be negotiating! Whether you end up with a yes often depends on how persistent you are.

PERSUASIVENESS

The power of persuasion is a boon to any negotiator. You will recall that negotiation is a form of persuasive communication. It is a way of getting others to do what you want them to do. How successful you are at persuading your counterpart depends on three factors:

1. **Credibility**

   Do you look the part, sound knowledgeable and confident, have relevant experience or expertise, and enjoy a good reputation? Do you represent an organization that possesses these qualities?

2. **Logic**

   Do you have facts, evidence, and statistics on your side? Is your reasoning sound? Can you point to specific examples that support your position?

3. **Emotion**

   Do you speak with passion and conviction? A dynamic and enthusiastic presentation is more persuasive than a dry one. Can you identify your counterpart's hot button? Their emotional driver might be ego, greed, fear—something other than the desire for a "good deal" by some objective or dollar-based measure.

Imagine coming home one day and seeing your neighbor in his driveway. A shiny new Mercedes is parked in the space where his old Toyonda used to sit. You say, "That's a beautiful car! Why did you decide to buy a Mercedes this time?" Of course you know why: it's about status, prestige, impressing people, flaunting his wealth, and other emotional and ego needs. But he will never admit it. He will offer a logical reason instead: it's a high performance machine, it has German engineering, it's a safe, solid car that will last for years, it will hold its value, etc.

People decide based on their emotions and justify their decisions with reason. The fact is that successful businesspeople are as emotionally driven as anyone, but they don't usually admit it. It is important for them to appear rational. So, make an emotional appeal to move your counterpart, but provide him with a logical hook to hang his hat on.

PEOPLE SKILLS

Having good people skills is a source of power for a win-win negotiator. It's essential to communicate clearly and smoothly. You need to show concern and respect for the other party and value your relationship. You must empathize with him, even when you do not agree.

It also helps to be likable. Smile, be friendly and approachable, and take a personal interest in your counterpart. Some people truly believe that they can keep warm and fuzzy feelings from influencing them during a hard-nosed business negotiation, but the best negotiators know better!

We will look more closely at people skills in the next chapter.

LEVERAGE

While the terms leverage and power are often used interchangeably, leverage is not the same as power. Traditional sources of power are fairly clear cut: information, expertise, resources, and so on are easy to identify and understand. Not so with leverage. Leverage is dynamic, it changes with the situation.

Leverage is largely a matter of perception. If you have the upper hand based on objective measures but don't know it, then you don't have it. And because the balance of power may shift as the negotiation progresses, you need to reassess it continually as you get new information or insights.

I like to think of leverage as who has the upper hand at a given time. This is determined by a number of factors, such as:

- Who needs the deal more. If the other party knows you need it, they have the upper hand. "Needs" can be intangible, such as ego, a need for consistency with social norms, or an emotional attachment. For example, if you tell the car dealer "This is my dream car! How much?" don't expect a discount.

- Who has more to lose. People hate to lose more than they love to win, so your counterpart may have an edge if you are playing it safe. Insurance agents often play this card.

- Who has less time. If you are up against a tight deadline, your counterpart may have the advantage. Time is money, and lack of time is desperation.

- Who has less control of the status quo. If you are able to call the shots or throw a wrench into the works, you may use this to your advantage.

- Who has a better Plan B. Developing a strong Plan B is arguably the single most important thing you can do to prepare for a negotiation. It allows you to walk away easily. On the other hand, if your Plan B is poor and your counterpart knows it, they have the upper hand. As your Plan B is so crucial, we will look at it in detail.

DEVELOPING AND USING YOUR PLAN B

One of the main themes of this book is that you must prepare well for a negotiation. So far, we've discussed how you need to gather information, study the negotiating environment, consider your interests and currencies, anticipate your counterpart's interests and currencies, and develop a range of options. You will also need to formulate a strategy, and understand and anticipate tactics and counter-tactics. While this is excellent advice, it is no guarantee that you and your negotiating partner will reach a satisfactory agreement.

You have limited control over the process and eventual outcome. There are just too many variables that you cannot control. Information is limited and imperfect. Situations change. Strategies and tactics fail. Emotions, ego, and irrationality affect human behavior. All you can do is your best.

And have a backup plan.

ALWAYS HAVE A PLAN B

Whenever you prepare to negotiate, ask yourself how you can best satisfy your interests if you and your negotiating partner are unable to reach an agreement. Can you satisfy your interests somewhere else? If so, with whom? Under what terms and conditions? Before you begin to negotiate, always have a viable backup plan, or a Plan B.

Suppose you are engaged in a difficult negotiation. Your counterpart is driving a hard bargain, and you are beginning to feel that you may have to settle for less than you would like. What can you do? The answer depends on your Plan B.

Negotiation is a consensual process, based on mutual agreement. You do not have to accept any offer unless you choose to. You can always say no. But we negotiate to satisfy some interest, and if we do say no, we must find another way to satisfy that interest.

In everyday jargon, we use the terms option and alternative interchangeably. In the negotiation context, however, it is useful to distinguish between options and alternatives. An option is a possible solution to a negotiation. During a negotiation, there is often a range of options or possible agreements available to satisfy your interests. But if you and your negotiating counterpart cannot agree on one, you may have to look elsewhere for an alternative means of getting what you need. These alternatives exist outside of the negotiation. So in negotiating parlance, an option is a possible agreement with your current negotiating counterpart, while an alternative would be a possible agreement with someone outside of the current negotiation.

For example, suppose you are negotiating for a salary increase with your current boss at Myco. You and your boss have a number of options available: she can offer you a big increase, no increase, or an increase of any number of figures in between. She can base the increase on your performance, the cost of living, or tie it to company practices or industry trends. She can offer you various combinations of benefits in lieu of a higher salary. These are all options that can result in a negotiated agreement.

If you and your boss cannot reach an agreement, you still have a choice: you can accept what your boss offers, or you can resign. What, then, are your alternatives? How can you satisfy your interests (recognition of your worth, maintaining your standard of living, being treated with fairness and respect, among other things) outside of Myco? You can find a position with another company, change careers, resume your studies, retire early, start your own business, or run away and join the circus. You may not like any of these alternatives, but you do have choices.

Some of your alternatives are better than others. When evaluating the options available with your negotiating counterpart, you just need to know which of the various alternatives available to you is the most attractive. This is your Plan B.* You then choose between what your counterpart is offering you and your Plan B. In the example given, if your best alternative is to find a similar position with another company, you can forget about joining

---

* Readers familiar with negotiation terminology may recognize my Plan B as the BATNA, or "Best Alternative To a Negotiated Agreement," developed by Roger Fisher and William Ury in their landmark book, *Getting to Yes* (1981). With all due respect to Professor Fisher, who was my first negotiation teacher, I dislike the term BATNA for two reasons:

First, the term is unwieldy. I often have students in my negotiation classes who have had previous negotiation training and have a vague recollection of the term. Most of them cannot recall what the letters stand for, let alone the meaning. Plan B is pretty intuitive, everyone gets it.

Second, the term is misleading. Suppose I am negotiating with you to buy your car. If we can't agree, what is my best alternative? I wouldn't *steal* the car from you, though that is clearly an alternative to a negotiated agreement. I would most likely negotiate an agreement to buy a similar car from someone else, which doesn't sound like much of an alternative, it's almost the same thing! (I understand, "alternative" has a specific meaning here, but if people can't remember the acronym they probably won't remember the special meaning either.) If you're a purist, feel free to think that the "B" in Plan B stands for BATNA.

the circus for the moment. Your decision then becomes: should I accept my boss's offer and stay with Myco, or do I take a job with Other Company?

If Other Company has not offered you a job, then you do not have that alternative. Your best alternative then might be to start your own business. If that is not particularly attractive to you, you would do well to find a better alternative. If you have no good alternatives when you ask your boss for that raise, you will have little power in the negotiation. You will have to accept what she offers, or resign.

THE POWER OF A STRONG PLAN B

Without a backup plan, you have very little negotiating power. With an attractive alternative, you have great power, even if your counterpart is a large, wealthy corporation. What traditionally passes for power—money, resources, an impressive title with a large organization, and other trappings of power—is no guarantee of success in negotiation. Other sources of power, such as information, preparation, and expertise, can tilt the balance of power in favor of the little guy. A strong Plan B is perhaps the greatest source of power of all. This source of power is largely a function of information and preparation.

Your Plan B is critical for a number of reasons:

- **Your Plan B gives you confidence**
  Your Plan B is like a safety net. If you can get a better outcome in the negotiation, take it; if not, walk away from the table and go with your Plan B. It *guarantees* that you will not be worse off by negotiating.

NEGOTIATING POWER AND YOUR PLAN B   101

- **Your Plan B is a benchmark**

  Most of the time, your Plan B is not very different from an option on the negotiating table. For example, your Plan B may be an offer for a position with Other Company at $3,500/month and you are negotiating with Myco for a similar position at a comparable salary. Knowing your Plan B gives you an idea of what a realistic option should be.

  While we usually find it easier to compare numbers, don't focus solely on dollars. Other Company may offer to pay you more than Myco, but you may have to work longer hours, have a longer commute, and they may offer you less attractive benefits. Consider all the pros and cons carefully when comparing your counterpart's offer with your Plan B.

- **Your Plan B must be realistic**

  It should be something you could and would really do if the negotiation fails. Bluffing, that is, claiming to have a Plan B that does not exist, can be risky. If you are negotiating a salary increase with your boss at Myco and you tell her that Other Company has offered you $1,000 more, she just might say "A thousand dollars more? That's great! You should take it!"

  Don't deceive yourself by fantasizing about an alternative that you wouldn't actually exercise. For example, suppose you have no competing offer and you decide your best alternative is to start your own business. That would require capital, a business plan, a considerable amount of effort, a healthy bank balance to tide you over for several months, some quantum of risk, and so on. If you are not prepared to accept these challenges, this is not your Plan B. Stop dreaming and develop a realistic Plan B.

- **Your Plan B can be improved**

  Your Plan B is not set in stone. For example, suppose your Plan B is an offer for a position with Other Company at $3,500 a month. All things being equal, you would not accept an offer from your boss for less than that figure. If Myco offers you $3,600 you take it; if they offer you less, you go with Other Company. But what if, during your negotiations with Myco, you contact Other Company and they agree to increase their offer to $3,800 plus insurance coverage and a transportation allowance? Or you get an offer from ThirdCo at $3,900? Now you can confidently ask Myco for more, knowing you can beat their previous offer of $3,600. Once you determine your Plan B, see if you can improve on it.

THE DANGER OF YOUR BOTTOM LINE

In Chapter 3 we saw that many negotiators decide upon the "worst" deal they are willing to accept before they begin negotiating. The rationale is that it is better to think about this coolly and objectively before the heat of the negotiation sways them to accept a poor offer. This sounds prudent, and a bottom line can offer some protection against making a bad deal.

However, a bottom line that looked good before the negotiation may prove unworkable during the negotiation. As offers and counter-offers are made, new information comes to light, new interests and currencies are identified, and situations change in various ways, the old bottom line may no longer be realistic. By its very nature, a bottom line is rigid; there's no point in having a bottom line that can change!

A bottom line is an arbitrary point. It may have been based on interests as understood at one time, but those interests can change or prove to have been misjudged as the negotiation proceeds. The bottom line figure resembles more of a position than a reflection of interests. Recall that a position is what you think you want, and an interest is what would really serve your needs.

Your bottom line is just a number, or an arbitrary position that may not be meaningful. Your Plan B is a better point of reference. It is a real alternative to a real option on the table. Therefore, you should compare the option before you (a possible solution to the negotiation) with your Plan B (your best alternative solution outside of this negotiation) and decide which one is better for you.

DEVELOPING YOUR PLAN B

Focus on your key interests and ask yourself how you might satisfy them if you cannot reach an agreement with the other party. List as many alternatives as you can think of. Remember, you are not looking for options—possible solutions to this negotiation—at this time. You are looking for alternatives outside of this negotiation, courses of action you could pursue with other parties or on your own. List the pros and cons for each. Which alternative is most favorable? Is it realistic? If so, this is your Plan B.

Your Plan B is your best alternative at a given point in time. But times change. You can also change your backup plan.

You can improve your Plan B or find a new one. There is no need to cling to your original Plan B throughout the negotiation—you can continue to improve it even as you negotiate. The better your Plan B, the better the agreement you can expect from your negotiating counterpart.

WHAT IS THEIR PLAN B?

Remember that your counterpart also has a Plan B. You may be able to estimate his Plan B by anticipating his alternatives to dealing with you and identifying the most favorable one. Put yourself in his shoes and try to determine his best alternative.

Just as you may be able to estimate your counterpart's Plan B, he may have some idea what your Plan B is as well. In our earlier example, your boss may know what Other Company and ThirdCo pay their employees.

DIMINISHING THEIR PLAN B

While Plan Bs can be improved, they can also be made to appear less attractive. The idea is to improve your Plan B and suggest that your counterpart's is weaker than he thinks it is. Of course, you need to be subtle and tactful about this. You also need to understand that your counterpart may use this tactic on you. However, if your Plan B is realistic and strong enough, you can resist this.

Returning to our example, suppose your boss says she can only increase your salary to $3,700. What is her best alternative if you resign? She may be able to hire a younger person for less than what she was paying you. Her Plan B looks good, perhaps even better than giving you a raise! How can you make it look weaker?

You can suggest that it will be troublesome and expensive to recruit a replacement for you. The new hire will take time before he can get up to speed and be productive. He may not work out at all and your boss will be back at square one, so why take the risk? Now her Plan B doesn't look so good, and she might decide to increase her offer. Alternatively, she might try to diminish your Plan B by suggesting that the managers at Other Company are slave drivers and they have a dysfunctional culture, so why leave your friends and a good position for a lousy couple of hundred dollars more?

There are other ways of making a Plan B seem less attractive. Suppose you are negotiating to purchase a house. Your offer of $372,000 is a bit less than what the seller would like. What is the seller's Plan B? Perhaps another prospect has expressed a willingness to buy the house for $374,500. What can you do to weaken his Plan B? Put down a cash deposit. The other prospect's words may sound sweeter, but they are only words, and money talks. The seller's Plan B suddenly seems less attractive next to your cold, hard cash.

WALKING AWAY

Psychologically, it may be difficult to walk away from a negotiation. You have invested time, effort, money, and psychic energy, and you don't want all of that to be for nothing. You may feel that your constituents are counting on you to reach an agreement, and they would be disappointed if you came back without one. You may feel pressure from the other party to "do your part" to make the deal happen. You may even look at your bottom line and decide that it was too unrealistic after all, and accept a proposal you should rule out.

Whenever you feel these pressures, focus on your interests! Remember that whatever resources you have invested are sunk costs and are irrelevant in evaluating whether an agreement makes sense at this time. Your constituents may be expecting an agreement, but after the fog clears they will be more disappointed with a bad one than none at all. The approval of your counterpart is not usually a valid consideration, so do not feel pressure to conclude an agreement just for his sake. Your bottom line may offer some protection against accepting a bad deal, but it may be too rigid in light of new information and currencies that come up during the course of the negotiation.

Do not use any of these factors to determine whether to conclude an agreement. The only thing to consider is your Plan B. Compare the best option on the table with your Plan B and decide which serves your interests better.

Having a strong Plan B is an indispensable part of preparing for your negotiation. A strong Plan B ensures that you will not settle for less than what you can get elsewhere, and gives you confidence that you can reach a more favorable agreement during a negotiation. By improving your Plan B and undermining your counterpart's Plan B, you can expect an even better outcome.

Negotiation is a voluntary process. No deal at all is better than a bad deal. You can walk away from a bad deal, but it is easier to walk away if you have a Plan B waiting for you. *Always* have a Plan B. If you don't, you're not ready to negotiate.

NEGOTIATING WITH A MONOPOLY*

This is one of the toughest puzzles in negotiation: how do you negotiate with a monopoly supplier when you need him but he doesn't need you? The problem seems insurmountable at first glance, but recall that "need" comes in many forms. Do you really need them in the true sense of the word, or is it really just a matter of convenience or preference?

In addition, a monopoly may take many forms. There's the pure monopoly you learned about (or slept through) in ECON 101, where one company really does control the entire supply (such as an electricity provider). More often, we're dealing with a seeming monopoly based on supply dependency. Your supplier may behave like a monopoly because there are high transition costs or barriers to leaving them, for example, the company that developed your software. Or your supplier may have access to your intellectual property or other critical information that binds you to them.

In all of these cases, we see the importance of preparation. How well do you understand your supplier's situation? How much does your business mean to them in dollars or as a percentage of

---

*   Based on Paranikas, Whiteford, Tevelson, and Belz, "How to Negotiate with Powerful Suppliers," *Harvard Business Review*, July–August 2015.

their overall business? Who are their other customers, and how do you compare? What are your supplier's strategic goals and future direction, and do these suggest any opportunities for you?

While there is no sure-fire answer that will work in every situation, there are a number of possible solutions that might work for you in a particular situation. Or for your boss. Most of these tactics can only be used at a senior level. We consider them here from easier to riskier.

1. Create new value for the supplier
Help the supplier enter new markets or industries
A good introduction is valuable. Can you bring your counterpart a new opportunity? For example, a beverage company had only one supplier available for packaging in a particular market and was being squeezed. However, the beverage maker was able to use that supplier in a couple of other markets where it had not been able to gain a foothold previously. The supplier gave across-the-board price concessions in exchange for getting contracts in the new market.

Help the supplier reduce its business risk
Recall that allocation of risk is a currency that can be monetized. For example, if your supplier's business is cyclical, you may be able to lock in a long-term contract at a lower price. The supplier may not *need* you, but they will benefit from your business during the slow part of their cycle. Your ability to help smooth out their ups and downs is a currency you have that they value and are willing to pay for.

2. Change the way you buy
Consolidate orders or bundle purchases

Your supplier may have a monopoly on some products or services, but they may have competition in other areas. Their desire to keep your business in those areas may make them behave more reasonably in others. You may be able to consolidate your orders with other business units of your organization. You may also form a consortium with other buyers and consolidate your purchases.

Review whether you need everything you're buying

For example, you may have purchased a high-end package with all the bells and whistles, only to discover that you don't use all the extras. Consider whether you could do with a lesser quantity or a more basic version. You may either save money by buying less, or motivate the supplier to give you a better rate for the whole package.

3. Create a new supplier
Bring in a new supplier from another market

This is a variation of the first scenario, above. Instead of the beverage company introducing their packaging provider to a new market in exchange for price concessions, they could have brought in a packager from another industry or geographic market to compete with their existing monopolist.

Vertically integrate

Rather than succumb to your monopoly supplier, consider whether you can produce it in-house, or acquire a company or hire the talent that can. Elon Musk has done this several times at SpaceX. He originally planned to buy old rockets from Russia.

When he couldn't reach an agreement with them, he started building his own rockets. When the company that fabricated the nose cones gave him a hard time, he started building his own nose cones. He did the same thing with fuel valves—very few companies can make such specialized valves, and SpaceX is now one of them.

When I relate this example to my students, I sometimes get a reply to this effect: "Sure, Elon Musk can do that, he's a billionaire, he's the CEO, etc. I can't do that at my company." My reply to that is: "Is Musk able to do it because he's a billionaire CEO, or is he a billionaire CEO *because he is able to do it?*" If you do not have the authority to make such a decision, maybe your real job is to persuade your bosses to do it.

4. Play hardball
Threaten to withhold or cancel orders
Your supplier may have a lot of leverage in terms of extracting a high price from you, but recall that leverage is a function of timing, and the balance may change. You might let them know that if they can't give you a better deal on this business, then you won't consider them for other business that might arise in the future. This may seem harsh, so consider it carefully. It also helps to have a specific piece of business in mind, so they appreciate the consequences.

Threaten to litigate
This is the nuclear option. Sue them (or threaten to sue them) for anti-competitive practices. Most of the legal regimes in the world's developed countries do not look kindly on monopolies

or restraints of trade, and the prospect of litigating might make the chance to squeeze a bit more out of you seem less appealing. If nothing else, it sends a strong signal that you're up against the wall, and even a powerful monopoly would rather have your business than lose it.

In short, no one holds all the cards—there are too many cards! Your seemingly powerful negotiating counterpart has problems and weaknesses of his own, and you may have currencies and leverage you are not aware of. If you don't see a way to deal with your monopoly, it doesn't mean there isn't one—it just means you haven't found it yet.

CHAPTER 5

COMMUNICATION AND RELATIONSHIP ISSUES

"Be soft on the people, hard on the problem."
— Roger Fisher and William Ury

THE IMPORTANCE OF MAINTAINING RELATIONSHIPS

There was a time not long ago when business was a jungle. Negotiating was very competitive, a win-lose affair. Businessmen ate each other for lunch. The strong survived, and a killer instinct was prized. That was the norm.

In the old days, railroads swallowed one another whole. Today, airlines form alliances, share codes, and recognize one another's frequent flyer miles. McDonald's sells Coca-Cola in its stores and gives away Disney toys. Computer makers pack their wares with the products of other companies—Intel, Microsoft, and so on. These are not casual flings, they are more akin to marriages. Both parties are in it for the long term.

It isn't just the business world that has become more interdependent. Countries are finding more and more reasons to collaborate. A continent that has historically been plagued with wars has now joined the European Union. A rising China, formerly mistrusted by the West, is welcomed into the world community.

Times have changed. Sure, there are still plenty of tough guys out there who still follow the laws of the jungle, but their days are numbered. There may also be one-off negotiations where you just want a quick win and don't particularly care how your counterpart fares. No one is holding a gun to his head, and he can choose whether to make a deal or not. However, these occasions are now the exception rather than the rule.

An interdependent world requires collaboration. It demands win-win outcomes. Relationships are important, and at the heart of any relationship is communication.

THE WINDOW OF OPPORTUNITY

First impressions are formed quickly and set the tone for the relationship that follows. We usually form an impression of someone within four seconds or four minutes of our first contact, depending on which expert you consult. In any event, it is more likely a matter of seconds than minutes. People make a judgment about you based on your appearance, your voice, and elements of non-verbal communication such as your posture and gaze. They will form an impression of you when they first speak with you on the phone or read your first e-mail to them.

Unfair, isn't it? You may not be at your best at your first contact. Your e-mail may have one or two typos. But you will still be judged on this limited and possibly misleading information. The good and the bad all go into the mix, and shape the perceptions that others form of you. While it may not be fair, you can do your best to use it to your advantage rather than let it hurt you. This window of opportunity is narrow, so make the most of it.

How can you increase the odds that others will form favorable impressions of you? How can you convey the image you wish to communicate, before you even say "Hello"? How can you project a positive image with someone you have never met? Here are my suggestions:

- First of all, you need to decide on the image you wish to project. What qualities should a first-rate negotiator possess? No doubt confidence, competence, preparedness, and professionalism rank high on that list. Strive to project these qualities.

- Make a grand entrance. Walk tall, with confidence and purpose, like you own the place. You want people to see that you are comfortable in your surroundings. Do not meander aimlessly or look around like you're confused or nervous.

- Look like a winner. Your appearance is critical. Dress better than the average person in your position. Make sure you are well-groomed. Have a nice pen, and keep your documents in an elegant bag or portfolio. This shows you are organized and attentive to detail.

- Make the first move. Don't wait for the other person to make the call; pick up the phone. Introduce yourself or greet her first. People respect those who take the initiative.

- Use a firm and friendly handshake. Make sure your hand is dry, and use a firm grip. Smile warmly and make eye contact. Radiate warmth, sincerity, and enthusiasm. Let the other person know you are happy to see him.

- Use a confident voice. You don't want to sound loud and arrogant, nor do you want to speak too softly. Speak in a measured, deliberate, and self-assured tone. Avoid fillers and erratic pauses that suggest uncertainty or hesitation. Do not end sentences with an upward inflection that sounds like a question. Use a slower pace as this sounds more authoritative than a faster one. Be calm and in control.

- Have an opening line ready. Know what you want to say, then say it clearly and confidently. Do not fumble over your words—it makes you sound unsure of yourself and your ideas seem half-baked.

- Be professional. Keep your promises, arrive for appointments on time, and follow up on tasks. Treat others with courtesy and respect, whether they are the CEO, the receptionist, or the janitor. Be honest and maintain your integrity.

THE HALO EFFECT

First impressions are necessarily based on limited and imperfect information. Because we want to know more, we tend to generalize and stereotype a person's characteristics based on whatever information we have available. We extrapolate the person's positive qualities and extend them to other areas of their personality. For example, if our counterpart is confident, articulate, and well dressed, we might assume he is also trustworthy, knowledgeable, and professional, *even though we have no sound basis for doing so!* This is how con men cheat their victims! This tendency to generalize favorable qualities is called the "halo effect." The halo effect is a shortcut we often take along the way to getting to know someone.

Studies have shown that teachers often assume that more attractive students are also more intelligent, and evaluate them accordingly. Those with more appealing names also receive preferential treatment. Businessmen who look like a million bucks get more upgrades on airlines and at hotels than their casually dressed colleagues. It may not be fair but it happens all the time, so make the most of it! If you increase the number of favorable qualities you project, you will also increase the probability that others will form a more positive impression of you.

The opposite is also true. Psychologists call this the "reverse-halo" or "horn effect" (as in the devil's horns). If we see some negative qualities in a person—such as a sloppy appearance, papers in disarray, and lack of familiarity with the details—we might assume she is also lacking in other areas. Maybe she is, or maybe she just lacks the level of polish, confidence, and social skills you expect. Or maybe she's just having a bad day.

To minimize the dangers of the halo effect or the horn effect, take your time in getting to know your counterpart, test your assumptions, and seek additional information. Hone your intuition. Keep your own halo bright and shiny, but be cautious in reading your counterpart.

You cannot control the impressions others will have of you, but you can influence them. Do what you can with the factors that are easiest to control, such as your clothing, grooming, accessories, behavior, voice, and other non-verbal communication. Project confidence, competence, preparedness, and professionalism. Let these bright spots create a shiny halo that lets others see you in the best light. Leverage your best qualities to enhance the way people perceive you in other areas as well.

What if the person you are dealing with does not have a positive first impression of you?

Can you salvage the situation? Yes, but it may be an uphill climb. Begin by addressing the problem directly. Apologize if warranted, and explain if you think it will help. Take responsibility. Everyone makes mistakes or has an off day, and most people are willing to let you make amends if you appear sincere. Work hard to win back their trust and confidence.

COMMUNICATE CLEARLY

Use simple language to reduce the risk of misunderstandings. Do not try to impress with big words when common, everyday words will do. Do not use slang, abbreviations, or jargon that your counterpart may not understand. When in doubt, decide in favor of simplicity. Ask to make sure, but be careful not to ask in a condescending tone.

Speak clearly and enunciate well. If you speak quickly, slow your pace down to match your counterpart's. If you have reason to believe your counterpart might not understand your accent or pronunciation, ask him to let you know if he is unsure about anything you may say. Many people feel awkward asking someone they don't understand to repeat what they said, or to speak more slowly, or to spell a word. Be proactive about avoiding miscommunications.

Be familiar with the jargon of your industry as well as your counterpart's industry. You may not understand corporatese or legalese or computerese. If you do not understand a term or expression, ask for clarification. Never pretend you understand something when you don't. You may just end up agreeing to something you don't want!

Even when not using jargon, do not assume you understand what your counterpart is saying. Paraphrase his statements and ask questions to clarify meaning.

SHOW RESPECT

Treat your counterpart with respect. Listen to her without interruption. Do not use an arrogant or condescending tone when speaking to her. Thank her for her time and input, and recognize any contributions that she makes.

You can also show respect by being polite and courteous. People like to hear "please" and "thank you." Invite your counterpart to precede you through the door. If you are the host, offer your guest coffee, tea, or other refreshment. Try to anticipate her needs and be accommodating. If you are the guest, make an appreciative comment about your host or her office. You want to be seen as pleasant and likable in your counterpart's eyes.

If your counterpart is from another country or culture, learn something about his values and customs. Ask questions that show a sincere interest and desire to learn about him as an individual. This shows you value him as a person and will help to put him at ease. As a result, communication will flow better, and intentions are less likely to be misinterpreted.

CREATE RAPPORT

Rapport means putting another person at ease and making a real connection. You must aim for this right from the beginning—it is a big part of laying the foundation. Be polite, friendly, and welcoming. Make small talk. Use the person's name. Smile. Offer him a drink or do him a small favor. Set a friendly tone and establish a collaborative working dynamic.

The essence of rapport is similarity and harmony. When two people are truly in rapport, their tone, pace, rhythm, volume, and many elements of their body language will be similar. This will occur naturally, though you can encourage the process by consciously mirroring elements of your counterpart's vocal quality and body language. Position yourself at his level—sit if he is sitting, and stand if he is standing. Use body language beyond the basic eye contact, smile, and handshake to create a feeling of similarity.

You can also emphasize similarity and encourage rapport by adopting similar vocabulary as the other party. If she tends to use certain expressions, use them yourself. She will notice, perhaps subconsciously, that there is something about you that she likes. People like people who are like themselves, so you want to be like the person you are with.

ASK QUESTIONS

Win-win negotiators ask a lot of questions. While asking questions is a good way to get the information that is critical for a win-win, this is not the only purpose served by asking questions. Asking questions helps you build rapport, gain thinking time, control the pace and direction of the discussion, clarify understanding, and persuade the other party. Of course, it is also a good way to gather information.

Asking questions will help you to achieve the following.

Build rapport

People generally engage in small talk when meeting someone new, or when encountering someone they haven't seen in a while. They usually ask mundane questions or make simple statements that invite response, such as "How are you?", "Nice weather we've been having.", "Think it'll rain?", and "Did you see the game last night?"

These questions are not designed to elicit useful information. No one cares about the weather except farmers, and I can poke my head out the window and see if it looks like rain myself. We ask these trite questions just to acknowledge that another human being is present, to interact with him at a basic level, to put him (and ourselves) at ease.

A win-win negotiator will ask questions and make small talk to be friendly and to get his counterpart to warm up to him. He wants to be likable. He knows that other people are more likely to agree with him if they like him. Cold and aloof negotiators do not fare as well as warm and friendly ones.

Gain thinking time

Asking questions is a good way to buy time. While the other party is responding, you can ponder a difficult point. Try to do this during pauses in the conversation, as you don't want to miss anything important while you are thinking. Use questions to slow down the pace of the negotiation and gather your wits.

Control the discussion

If you have ever observed a trial lawyer conducting a cross-examination, or an interrogator grilling a suspect, you know how questions can be used to control a conversation. You can ask questions to steer the conversation in the direction you want it to go, to follow your agenda. It's better to be the one asking the questions than the one in the hot seat.

Clarify understanding

Win-win negotiators ask questions to test their assumptions and confirm their understanding. Ask a direct question if you are not absolutely sure about something, even if you think you are pretty sure about it. Better safe than sorry.

Persuade the other party

We negotiate to persuade another person to do what we want him to do. People often react defensively when confronted with a direct statement. For example:

"I'm going to need it delivered by Friday."

"Sure, everybody wants it yesterday, we're already stretched to the limit, you'll just have to wait."

Instead, use questions to suggest the answer you want.

"Is there any way we could have it delivered by Friday?"

"Well, let's see. If you can sign off on the copy by this afternoon we might be able to expedite it."

Of course, there are no guarantees you will get the answer you want, but using questions skillfully is more persuasive than telling people what you want them to do.

Gather information

Open-ended questions are very general and encourage the other party to talk. They usually begin with what, why, or how. As such,

COMMUNICATION AND RELATIONSHIP ISSUES 123

they should be your focus, especially during the early stages of laying the foundation of the negotiation. Open-ended questions show concern about the other's interests and a willingness to listen. They also help establish rapport.

There are many possible and unpredictable answers to open-ended questions. The answers may give you the information you were seeking, but they often contain additional, unanticipated, and potentially valuable information as well. They open up the field of inquiry, providing a wide variety of information for you to explore. Occasionally you will get some information that can be a game changer.

Closed or leading questions are very specific. They lead people to where you want them to go. The answers are often predictable, usually a simple yes or no. Closed questions are good for establishing facts, confirming understanding, gaining commitment, and summarizing. Thus, they are especially useful in the later stages of a negotiation.

Follow-up or probing questions allow you to dig for additional information and detail. They may be either open or closed. Whenever your counterpart gives you a vague, ambiguous, or incomplete answer—often with the intention of keeping you from pursuing an issue—press for more specifics with probing questions. Don't let him brush you aside.

When asking questions, be careful with the tone of your voice, the way you phrase your questions, and your body language. A sigh, or the sound of impatience or exasperation in your voice, can put the other person on the defensive and cause them to share less information. Use a warm, friendly tone when probing, for that will help you to get the answers you want.

Be especially careful with a naked why question. A why question can sound like an accusation, and puts the other party on the defensive. Find a way to turn it into a what or how question. For example:

- "Why did you do that?" [sounds harsh, accusing]
- "What prompted you to decide to do that?" [sounds softer, more sincere]

Ask a lot of questions—even if you think you know the answers—and listen to the answers carefully.

LISTEN

Western cultures value speaking over listening. We think more highly of men of words and action than those who sit quietly. Our companies reward those who express their opinions, not those who weigh the opinions of others. No wonder most of us prefer to speak than listen. This is not necessarily a good thing in a negotiation.

Most negotiators talk too much. They think they need to make their positions clear from the get-go, to make sure their counterpart knows what's what and is duly impressed. The most successful negotiators talk less than the other party. Let your counterpart do most of the talking. The more she talks, the more information you learn. You already know what you think—wouldn't it be great to know what your counterpart thinks? If you knew what she was thinking, what was important to her, and perhaps gleaned some useful insights by hearing her out, wouldn't that help you to negotiate a better outcome? If so, you need to listen and learn. And in particular you need to listen actively.

The following explains how to listen actively.

Paraphrase

Restate or paraphrase what the speaker has just said to test assumptions, clarify confusion, and confirm understanding. Seek to completely understand the substance of the message. Use phrases such as

- "If I understand you correctly …"
- "It seems like you really want …"
- "Am I correct in saying that you …"

Encourage the speaker

The more they talk, the more you learn. Use statements, words, or sounds to encourage the speaker to continue or elaborate:

- "I'd like to hear more about that."
- "Why is that?"
- "Really?" "No kidding!" "Unbelievable!"
- "Hmmm." "Uh huh!" "I see."

You can also use non-verbal signals to encourage the speaker, such as nodding your head in agreement, exhibiting appropriate facial expressions, leaning forward, maintaining an open and attentive posture, and mirroring the speaker's body language. Your objective is to get as much information as possible, and to understand your counterpart clearly.

Focus on red flag words

Red flag words are ambiguous words or phrases that cry out for elaboration. For example, the word "interesting" can mean "intriguing," or it can be a diplomatic way of saying "I don't like that idea much." Whenever your counterpart uses an ambiguous word, ask questions for clarification.

People choose their words for a reason. If you are not sure what they mean, ask them. Your counterpart may use certain words to avoid giving information. Learn to recognize these red flags and dig for the information your counterpart is reluctant to share. If you ask specifically, he will often tell you. For example:

"That's a very interesting proposal, Mr. Jones. However, I feel we could manage with our current configuration for the time being."

You should be thinking, and asking: "What do you mean by 'manage'? Is it not doing everything you expect? What is working well, and what would you like to see improve?" You could also seize on the phrase "for the time being" by asking, "How long are we talking about? What is your time frame? What other factors are affecting your time frame?"

EMPATHIZE

The only problem with active listening is that it can be mechanical. Animated figures at Disneyland also nod their heads in agreement and say, "I see." An active listener may be sincere, or he may not be. Sometimes it's hard to tell.

While active listening is a great start, there is an even higher level of listening: empathetic listening. Empathetic listening includes all of the above, plus another element: reflecting the speaker's emotional state. Knowing what others are feeling and showing them that you care is the essence of empathy. You must truly understand a person's feelings to reflect them—you can't fake it!

The renowned psychologist Carl Rogers described empathy as non-judgmentally entering another person's world. When you enter his world openly and see it as he sees it, you can truly understand him. You don't need to agree with him, just try to understand his point of view.

Lawyers have a saying that an agreement is a meeting of the minds. In other words, if you and I both have the same idea in mind, then we are in agreement. Imagine if we could not only have a meeting of the minds but a meeting of the hearts as well. If you could understand what I am thinking and also feel what I am feeling—that's empathy!

Empathetic listening also shows that you respect your counterpart and are interested in his views. It is a way of validating him as an individual, which tends to make him more favorably disposed towards you.

Take your listening to an even higher level. Strive to become an empathetic listener. Show empathy by identifying your counterpart's feelings and reflecting them. It isn't enough to care about the person—you must show her that you care. Ask yourself, *What emotion is behind that statement?*

Then respond with a statement or ask a question that reflects your counterpart's emotional state. For example:

"That must have been a big disappointment."

"I can see that you're frustrated."

"You must be worried about that. What are you going to do?"

This does wonders towards building rapport and trust, strengthening your relationship, and encouraging the flow of information. It also makes you more likable.

Note that empathizing does not mean agreeing. You can understand how your counterpart feels without agreeing with her position. She will appreciate your concern whether you agree with her or not. As the saying goes, people don't care how much you know until they know how much you care.

MIRRORING

Regardless of whether you are negotiating face to face or by telephone, you can use the mirroring technique. Mirroring is simply repeating the last few words of your counterpart's statement. When you do this, they tend to elaborate on whatever they just said. It is always good to keep your counterpart talking so that you get useful information. In addition, this helps create rapport and likability—people feel at ease when they hear someone else speaking their language. It produces a comforting sense of similarity. Here's an example:

Him: "Our last supplier had some reliability issues."

You: "Reliability issues …"

Him: "Yes, it was not unusual to get late shipments, and they weren't very responsive to our calls."

You: "They weren't responsive to your calls …"

Him: "No, we'd have to leave a few messages most of the time and chase them for an answer."

You: "I see. It seems responsiveness is important to you." [then discuss how you can do better]

As you can see, there is no set rule as to how many words you repeat, or how many consecutive replies you can do it for. Use your judgment. Just don't push it so far that they feel you are mimicking them. Once you have elicited enough information to feel comfortable with your next move, take the conversation in that direction.

FORCED EMPATHY

One of the qualities that separates the best negotiators from the rest is empathy—the ability to not only see things from your counterpart's perspective, but to truly understand that perspective. This is not easy for most people, who are largely if not exclusively focused on *their* position, *their* reasons, and what *they* want to say next. With empathy in such short supply, wouldn't it be great if you could *force* your counterpart to empathize with you? There is a way, and oddly enough it's called "forced empathy"!

Fisher and Ury relate the following anecdote:[*]

In 1970, an American lawyer had a chance to interview President Nasser of Egypt on the subject of the Arab-Israeli conflict. He asked Nasser, "What is it you want [Israeli Prime Minister] Golda Meir to do?"

Nasser replied, "Withdraw!"

"Withdraw?" the lawyer asked.

"Withdraw from every inch of Arab territory!"

"Without a deal? With nothing from you?" the American asked incredulously.

"Nothing. It's our territory. She should promise to withdraw," Nasser replied.

---

[*] Fisher and Ury, *Getting to Yes* (1981) p. 115.

The American asked, "What would happen to Golda Meir if tomorrow morning she appeared on Israeli radio and television and said, 'On behalf of the people of Israel I hereby promise to withdraw from every inch of territory occupied in '67: the Sinai, Gaza, the West Bank, Jerusalem, the Golan Heights. And I want you to know, I have no commitment of any kind from any Arab whatsoever.'"

Nasser burst out laughing, "Oh, would she have trouble at home!"

Understanding what an unrealistic option Egypt had been offering Israel may have contributed to Nasser's stated willingness later that day to accept a cease-fire ...

This is an example of forced empathy—making the other party see things from your point of view. President Nasser may have been fully convinced of the merits of his position, but once the lawyer asked the question of how his counterpart could agree to it, he realized the futility of his demand. He was forced to consider her point of view and take a more realistic approach.

The best way to force empathy is with a question, particularly a what or how question. A question forces the other party to engage. They will answer the question in their head if not out loud. It's almost impossible for a person asked a what or how question *not* to think about your position.

However, questions beginning with why won't usually work, as it sounds like an accusation and puts people on the defensive. Luckily, any why question can be converted into a what or how question. For example:

"Why did you do it that way?"—How would you feel if someone asked you this question? It sounds like they are accusing you, blaming you, or at the very least are unhappy about what you did. Most people would feel they were under attack and go on the defensive. It does not foster a positive negotiating atmosphere. You could always rephrase the question as a what or how question:

"What prompted you to do it that way?"—It sounds like you are curious about their thought process. This is a very different sensation than feeling besieged! You can also add an introductory phrase as a buffer, to make your question even more user friendly:

"I'm curious, how did you come up with that approach?"—This phrasing sounds like they are not only curious, but also favorably impressed!

Statements do not have the same effect as questions. They are more factual and don't have as much power to evoke empathy. A statement such as "Try to see it from my point of view" sounds impersonal and may cause resistance. Such statements can just be ignored. You want to make it visual, paint a picture in their mind. When you ask a what or how question, the other party imagines himself in your place and naturally thinks about your perspective. Here are some examples of questions that force empathy:

- What would you tell my boss if you were me?
- How am I supposed to do that?
- What would you do if you were in my position?
- What do we have to do to close this deal?
- How can we make this work?
- What will you do if we don't reach an agreement?
- What do you think would happen if …?

Remember that negotiation is about give and take. Forcing the other party to empathize with you works best if you first empathize with them. If you are playing hardball and relentlessly pressing your agenda without any regard for their needs, they are less likely to be receptive. However, if you empathize with them first, the reciprocity principle kicks in and they will be much more inclined to consider your point of view.

THE ROAD TO YES PASSES THROUGH NO

We have been conditioned to prefer yes to no. Most people think they want a yes. Yes is good—it means you get what you want. No means rejection, and rejection hurts—but only if you take it personally. You shouldn't! There can be many reasons why they say no, and after all it is their choice. It is not necessarily a reflection on you. But even though we think we want a yes, yes doesn't always mean yes.

A yes that is too easy is usually fake. They say yes, but they mean "Yes, whatever, now leave me alone." They tell you what you want to hear just to make you go away. They are not agreeing to anything.

Sometimes, a yes is just a confirmation but not a commitment. It means, "Yes, I understand, uh huh, okay, right, I see." But it does not mean, "Yes, we have a deal!"

Of course, you ultimately want that last kind of yes—the commitment—but only at the end. The road to yes passes through no.

There's another reason you don't want to get a yes right away. A quick yes, too easily given, makes you wonder whether you really got a good deal. It leads to the winner's curse, where you think: *That was too easy. Why was he so quick to agree? Does he know something I don't? I think I've been had!* But a hard earned yes gained after a series of no's gives you confidence that you got close to the best deal possible.

A lot of salesmen have been trained to ask a series of simple questions to get the prospect to say yes, and then lead them to the big yes at the end. A lot of people have been led down that path of yeses before and they feel the pressure, but they rarely say yes. And if they do, it's usually a "Yes, whatever, now leave me alone" yes, or an "Okay, right, I understand" confirmation yes, but not a commitment yes.

When people feel pressure or are not sure what to do, they say no. No protects them. No maintains the status quo. No lets them stay in the driver's seat. When they say no, they are really saying "I'm not going to agree to anything you ask until I'm good and ready! I'm in control here!" So why not cut to the chase and let them say no? Let them feel safe and in control. It's not about getting a yes immediately; it's about getting a yes at the end: "Yes, we've got a deal!"

Every negotiation begins with a no. If it had been a yes you wouldn't be negotiating, would you? No is just the starting point, and yes comes at the end.

Most people get discouraged when they hear the word no, especially when it comes from a high power or high status person, such as a boss or an important client. They are afraid to pursue the matter because they don't want to be seen as being pushy or overbearing. Perhaps they imagine the other party thinking, *What part of NO don't you understand?* Sometimes, they just don't want to risk damage to their ego. After all, one no is bad enough. Why risk further rejection by asking again? Won't the answer be the same?

The word no is not carved in stone. Whenever you hear a no, treat it as an opening position. When someone tells you no, what they really mean is "Based on how you have framed your request, and on my mood, and on the alignment of the stars at this point in time, and various other factors too numerous to mention and which I do not fully understand anyway, I am inclined to say no for the time being. However, if you reframe your request, or modify your proposal, or ask me again later, or tomorrow, or next week, I might say yes." This is very different from a firm, final, absolute no, isn't it?

There are a lot of things your counterpart might be saying when he says no. A no can mean:

- I'm not sure …
- I'm afraid …
- Maybe I'm missing something …
- What if I make a mistake?
- What will my boss/stakeholders say when they see this deal?
- Maybe I'll get a better deal if I wait …
- I'm not ready to commit …
- If I say yes, then I'm agreeing to your proposal and you're in control and who knows what will happen; it's easier and safer for me to say no …

So the next time someone tells you no, ask "Why not?" They will reply "Because of A, B, and C." Depending on their reason, think about how you might change your approach. Modify your request to take A, B, and C into account, and present them with your new proposal. They will either say yes or no. If they say yes, congratulations! If they say no, ask "Why not?" They will reply "Because of D, E, and F." Modify your request. Bundle your request into a package of other issues. Explore other possibilities. You just may succeed in turning that no into a yes.

SUBSTANTIVE AND PERSONALITY ISSUES

In every negotiation there are substantive issues and personality issues. Substantive issues concern the subject of the negotiation. For example, issues such as price, quantity, delivery dates, payment schedules, and other terms and conditions are substantive issues. We bargain over these issues as we strive to reach an acceptable agreement.

There are also personality issues that enter any negotiation and affect the parties' relationship. Your counterpart may have certain habits and mannerisms that irritate you. Perhaps he is loud, insensitive, and intimidating. He may always arrive late, talk excessively, and keep you longer than expected. He may try to pressure you with hardball tactics or rush you into making a hasty decision. Or she may be very charming and try to sweet talk you into conceding more than you had planned. The following are my suggestions for dealing with substantive and personality issues.

Keep personality issues separate from substantive ones

It is easy to let our like or dislike of our counterpart influence the way we deal with him. If we like him, we may allow him more generous terms than we might otherwise. If we don't like him, we may let our feelings distract us from our interests. If we are intimidated by him, we may make concessions on some issues in the hope of winning his approval.

Separate the people from the problem. Do not let personality factors influence you. When a charming counterpart asks you for a concession, ask yourself whether you would make this concession to someone you don't like. Your response should be the same. Focus on the substance. A good deal is a good deal, regardless of the personality of your counterpart.

Do not make concessions on substantive issues in exchange for concessions on personality

Imagine you are negotiating with an intimidating counterpart. You might be tempted to offer a concession on price (substantive) in the hope of pacifying him. This will backfire. Instead of easing up, he will continue to be difficult in order to extract more substantive concessions from you, because you have shown him that it works! Rather than try to appease him, stand firm. Negotiate on the issues and focus on your interests. Tough negotiators respect strength and despise weakness. Do not make concessions on substantive matters to buy approval or make the relationship smoother. Trade substantive concessions only for other substantive concessions.

Say no to the request, not to the person

Bear in mind that people do not always distinguish the messenger from the message. Even though you may not intend for your refusal to be a personal rejection, some people will take it that way. Help them maintain perspective by being clear that you are rejecting the request and not the person making it. For example, say "I cannot agree to that condition" rather than "I cannot help you with that."

Give reasons

When rejecting a proposal, first say what you like about it. Look for common ground, a point of agreement. Then explain what you do not like about it, or what you would change, and why. People like to know why. Explaining your reasoning helps the other party to understand.

Avoid negative words and characterizations

Strong negative words are highly charged. Their impact can spread from the problem to the people. For example, using strong negative language to refer to a proposal may be taken personally by the speaker. Your characterization of their idea is taken as a personal slight or insult. In addition, if you use negative words they will make you appear as a negative or unlikable person. Stay neutral or positive.

BUILD TRUST

The foundation of any good negotiating relationship is trust. Negotiators who have a trusting relationship are able to reach better agreements in less time and with less formality. They are less likely to have disputes, and are more likely to resolve the disputes amicably when they do arise.

You can build a trusting relationship by getting to know your counterpart as an individual. Spend time socializing and getting to know one another informally. In some cultures this getting acquainted process is critical, and they won't get down to business until they feel comfortable with their counterpart.

Getting to know one another socially is not enough. You must also be trustworthy. You must earn and deserve another person's trust. This can be conceptualized in the form of an equation, where your trust quotient is a function of credibility, reliability, intimacy, and self-orientation:[*]

---

[*]   From David Maister, *The Trusted Advisor* (2000)

$$Trust = \frac{Credibility + Reliability + Intimacy}{Self\text{-}orientation}$$

Credibility refers to your knowledge, expertise, qualifications, and how effectively you communicate them to others. Why should the other party believe you or view you as an authority? Credibility is largely a matter of perception, and can be enhanced in the moment by how you dress, speak, and carry yourself. How can you appear more credible to your counterpart?

Reliability is about being able deliver what you promise. Are you able to exceed (or at least manage) your counterpart's expectations? Do you deliver what you promise? Better yet, do you have a reputation for under-promising and over-delivering? Note that you represent your organization. If your organization has a strong reputation, it may transfer to you and vice versa. A sterling reputation can do wonders, but a poor one can be hard to shake.

Intimacy refers to whether the other party feels comfortable or secure in dealing with you. It is a function of likability, rapport, and the quality of your relationship. How can you build your relationship so that your counterpart feels at ease with you?

Self-orientation is a matter of focus and intent. Are you clearly motivated by money and your own advantage? Does your counterpart feel you are there for them, or for yourself? How can you minimize the appearance of self-interest and temper it with empathy and concern for your counterpart's interests?

In order to increase your trust quotient, you can increase the values in the numerator (credibility, reliability, and intimacy), decrease the value of the denominator (self-orientation), or both. Here are some ways to develop your trustworthiness:

- **Be honest**—Keep your word and maintain a reputation for truthfulness.
- **Be transparent**—Being open and above board will allow others to trust you. This does not mean you have to tell them everything; it is perfectly acceptable to tell your counterpart that certain information is confidential.
- **Be consistent**—People are more comfortable with those who have a clear set of values and follow them without fail. Always under-promise and over-deliver.
- **Value the relationship**—In an ongoing relationship with a valued partner, the future of the relationship is more important than the outcome of any single negotiation. Make sure your counterpart knows you feel this way.
- **Be trusting**—Trust is a two-way street. If you want people to trust you, you have to show you trust them. You need not trust them blindly of course, but be willing to give them the benefit of the doubt (at least until they show you your trust in them is misplaced).
- **Temper your self-interest with fairness**—While everyone is expected to negotiate for their own benefit, pursuing only your interests to the exclusion of fairness will make you seem less trustworthy. Show a healthy regard for the interests of your counterpart as well.

While trust is a big plus, it is not essential in a negotiation. Even though you may not trust your counterpart, you can still negotiate fruitfully if you trust the process. Nations often negotiate with one another even when there is low trust because they trust the institutional framework of the international community. Similarly, your bank won't allow a lack of trust to stop them from giving you a loan. They have faith in the banking system, the credit reporting system, and the legal system. But as business and negotiation continue to become more relationship-oriented, trust will become increasingly valued.

NON-VERBAL COMMUNICATION

Non-verbal communication is often more important than words alone. Is your counterpart open and approachable, or defensive and secretive? Is he honest, or deceptive? Is he interested, eager, desperate, confused? Pay attention to the body language, tone of voice, and facial expressions of your counterpart. Much of this is intuitive, and you can improve your reading of basic non-verbal signals with awareness and practice. However, I believe the 80/20 rule applies here. For most everyday negotiators, it is not realistic to expect to become an expert at reading body language. You don't need to decode thousands of micro-expressions. You only need to be good enough. Most of your time and effort should be devoted to preparing for your negotiations.

However, it is useful to have a sense of whether your counterpart is uncomfortable, lying, or behaving in a way that is incongruent with what he is saying. If you do suspect something isn't right, try to find out why. You might try to label their emotion by saying something like:

- "I sense that you may not be comfortable with this term ..."
- "I may be wrong, but you seem to be unhappy about ..."
- "Did I say something to upset you?"

Your counterpart may or may not be forthcoming in his response. You can't control that, but it doesn't help to ignore the elephant in the room. In fact, he is likely to deny your suggestion to save face, but he may moderate his behavior in response.

In any event, it is up to you to decide whether to accept an agreement, regardless of whether you believe your counterpart lied about something or seemed to be acting funny. Your final agreement may take the form of a written contract with black-and-white language and no non-verbal communication whatsoever within the four corners of the document, but having some understanding of body language and facial expression can make getting there easier.

Non-verbal communication is a two-way street. Be aware of the non-verbal signals you are sending to others. Drumming your fingers on the table might suggest you are nervous or impatient. Arms crossed across your chest can signal that you are defensive or uncomfortable. Lack of eye contact suggests lack of confidence or deception. Avoid body language and facial expressions that convey weak or negative qualities. Use body language that suggests the qualities you want to project: confidence, competence, preparedness, and professionalism. The right body language can help keep your halo polished and gleaming.

Non-verbal communication is a field of its own, and it is extraordinarily difficult to master. It certainly cannot be covered in a few paragraphs. Those who do succeed in mastering it take years to learn the art. Rather than attempt to decode the nuances of other people's body language, it is more productive to focus on your own non-verbal communication. Ask a few close friends or colleagues to candidly assess you on your facial expression, gestures, and mannerisms. Have them video record you in a negotiation or meeting and watch yourself in action. It may not be pretty but you need to know the unvarnished truth. Are you unwittingly sending out the wrong signals? Are there any glaring deficiencies? Work on improving in those areas.

CULTURAL ISSUES

There are additional points to keep in mind when negotiating with people from other cultures. You need to be aware of cultural differences, but treat them as a working hypothesis rather than a given. You may have heard that Japanese businessmen do not like to say no, and often say yes when they have no intention of agreeing, but that does not mean *your* particular Japanese counterpart will follow that pattern. Avoid stereotyping. Also, remember that personality factors may or may not be in line with culture-based expectations. Treat each counterpart as an individual.

Globalization has had a homogenizing effect on many cultural elements. People are more aware of many cultural differences and tend to be accommodating. For example, in the past, a Japanese businessman would bow when greeting a counterpart, and a well-informed Western businessman would know enough to bow rather than shake hands. Today, most Japanese would shake hands, but if you bow, that would also be acceptable. You could do either or both without causing an international incident.

While gestures, customs, and other behaviors are widely known, there are still many not so obvious cultural differences you should be aware of. We will touch on some of the more important cultural dimensions of negotiating, but this is just scratching the surface. There are many books and even entire series of books on doing business in China, Egypt, Pakistan, etc. If you are going to one of those countries, or negotiating with someone from there, read the book for that country. Know before you go. If you have a colleague or contact from that country, or one who has experience dealing with that culture, ask her to tell you some of the more important do's and don'ts. It's also a good practice to learn a few basic phrases in the native language, such as good morning, please, thank you, etc., even if they customarily do business in English. Most people appreciate this greatly and it will help you start off on a positive note. And on that note, here are some of the more important cultural considerations you need to know:

High context vs low context of communication
In a high context culture, communication is subtle and highly nuanced. Words often express meaning indirectly, and a great deal of meaning is inferred. You must choose your words carefully, and understand that even precise words often take a back seat to custom, culture, context, and other elements of interpretation. Asian cultures tend to be more high context than Western ones.

In a low context culture, words are used plainly and directly. While this may support clear communication with other low context negotiators, it may seem blunt or even rude to a high context counterpart. Make sure you understand where your counterpart is on the context dimension.

Polychronic vs monochronic view of time

People of different cultures have different ideas about time. Growing up in Miami, I was exposed to the concept of "Cuban time." If you are thirty minutes late to a Cuban wedding, you will still be the first one there—everyone is expected to be late. Some Asian countries go by "rubber time," reflecting a more relaxed attitude towards time. Cultures that are more flexible about time and deadlines, and often tend to be slower paced, are said to be polychronic.

Monochronic cultures, on the other hand, value punctuality as a sign of respect and professionalism. If you are a few minutes late to a meeting, they might hold it against you. You can see how these differences in the way time is perceived could have an impact on a negotiation.

Formal vs informal

In a formal culture, protocols regarding title, role, seniority, social class, and even gender are important. Those who are perceived to be higher status have certain rights and privileges that must be recognized. In some of these cultures, younger people are not invited to speak until their elders have had their say, and women may not be a familiar sight in the boardroom.

In an informal culture, a more casual approach is acceptable. Age, gender, and class are not a major issue, and titles are not deemed important. A young person is likely to be treated according to his role and expertise, and not on the basis of age or inexperience. Think Silicon Valley.

Individual vs collective focus

Individualistic cultures have a strong focus on the individual. You are encouraged to go you own way, follow your muse, and self-actualize. Rebels are not only tolerated but encouraged and revered.

Collectivistic cultures emphasize one's role in the group, achieving consensus, and conformity. They value humility, and the nail that stands above the rest gets hammered down. Asian cultures are more likely to be collectivist, and in many of them the family name precedes the given name, reflecting the emphasis of the group over the individual. This is also changing quickly, and a new individualistic and entrepreneurial spirit is emerging in many traditionally collectivist societies.

High negotiation vs low negotiation

High negotiation cultures often have a pervasive haggling mindset where bargaining is expected. Think of a Middle-Eastern bazaar. People enjoy the thrill of the game, and fixed price transactions are not considered fun.

In a low negotiation culture, bargaining has a more limited role. Haggling may be seen as undignified. A customer from a low negotiation culture will be eaten alive in a souk.

The term "culture clash" can mean many things, but a large part
of it comes from these five dimensions of cultural context. The
situation on the ground is rapidly evolving with globalization, but
tradition dies hard. Try to anticipate what cultural issues might
arise when negotiating with a particular counterpart. Having
said that, don't put too much stock in stereotypes or cultural
caricatures. Individual characteristics are more important than
cultural attributes. Intention goes a long way. If you approach
your counterpart with universal human values, treat her with
respect, build rapport, and seek understanding, you should be
able to navigate any cultural differences.

NEGOTIATING BY TELEPHONE OR E-MAIL

Many people ask me if they should negotiate face-to-face, by
telephone, or through e-mail. In many instances, the answer
will be dictated by considerations of cost, location, timing, and
convenience. In other instances, you will have a choice.

Negotiating face-to-face is more formal, but fosters better
communication and understanding. It is a richer platform,
allowing you the benefit of observing facial expression, body
language, and other non-verbal cues. As a result, face-to-face
negotiation is more likely to result in a win-win outcome. This
makes it suitable for negotiating more substantial matters. The
more important the negotiation, the more desirable it becomes
to negotiate face-to-face.

Many negotiations are now conducted by e-mail. E-mail
communication is more likely to be misinterpreted than face-

to-face or telephone communication, but it might be the best choice for small matters, or where there are time, travel, or cost constraints. It also allows you to think about what you want to say and prepare a solid reply. If you are not quick-witted, assertive, or articulate, e-mail may be a better channel for you. However, negotiating by e-mail is slower, less fluid, and less likely to result in a win-win outcome.

Negotiating by telephone is a quick, low cost option. This channel ranks in between face-to-face meetings and e-mail exchanges in terms of clarity of communication. It is good for routine matters, or those not weighty enough to justify face-to-face contact.

There are a few other advantages to telephone negotiations:

- They take less time than face-to-face meetings. Sometimes, a simple face-to-face negotiation is drawn out simply to justify the time and effort required to travel to your counterpart's office.
- It is easier to say no over the phone. The telephone provides a buffer and eliminates the need to look into the eyes of the disappointed party.
- The telephone is less intimidating than face-to-face meetings for less assertive negotiators, so this helps the less powerful party. Disappointed eyes are bad enough, but an intimidating face is even harder to handle!
- It gives substance and logic more weight relative to style and form. There may be some pomp and circumstance in a face-to-face meeting, whereas a telephone negotiation allows you to cut to the chase.

There are now many tele- and video-conferencing platforms, with more popping up all the time. They are cheaper than international travel, but I don't recall being on many of such calls that went smoothly. Technology marches on, but communication issues will always be with us.

CHAPTER 6

PSYCHOLOGICAL PITFALLS: EMOTIONS AND BIASES

*"What makes humanity is not reason.
Our emotions are what make us human."*
— E.O. Wilson

Negotiation is widely thought to be a deeply rational process. Planning, preparation, strategizing, and trying to think several moves ahead as you try to outmaneuver your counterpart all suggest a highly logical brain at work. The reality is a less flattering interpretation of our analytical powers: we are creatures of emotion.

THE ROLE OF EMOTION IN NEGOTIATION

Emotions are always present in every human activity, including negotiation. We all have them, so we have to live with them—ours and theirs. Emotions affect the way we think, feel, and act. We cannot avoid them, so the best thing to do is recognize them and learn to deal with them constructively.

Some emotions are positive: joy, confidence, fun. Others are negative: anger, fear, embarrassment. Negative emotions tend to stimulate competitive impulses, which lead to a win-lose dynamic. Positive emotions encourage cooperation and support win-win outcomes.

Emotions are also contagious. We can spread them to—and catch them from—others. Generally, the person who expresses her emotions more forcefully will influence the one who is less expressive.

The implications for negotiation are straightforward. A win-win negotiator will manage the negative emotions in herself and not provoke them in others. She will also display positive emotions, and will say and do things that are likely to bring out positive emotions in others. Sounds simple enough, doesn't it? Unfortunately, it's not.

THE LANGUAGE OF EMOTION

Many people think of negotiation as a competition. Win-win negotiators think of it as an opportunity to collaborate and solve a common problem together. The language you use can support or detract from these mindsets, so it's important to choose your words wisely.

Words such as I, me, my, mine, you, your, and yours support a competitive negotiating dynamic. I and you contrast sharply and make it clear that we are at opposite ends of the spectrum. These words suggest that I will win and you will lose, or you will win and I will lose. It is difficult to reach a win-win outcome with a "me against you" mentality.

There may be times when you need to say I or you, but try to avoid these words whenever possible. Instead, try to use we, us, and our. These words express collaboration and suggest we are both on the same side, working together to solve our problem.

Using we and other collaborative language helps to set the tone for a win-win. However, when it does come down to I or you, an I statement works better than a you. For example:

> *"Your asking price is too high."*

This sounds judgmental, with an opinion masquerading as fact. There is also an implied criticism, which will put the other party on the defensive. He may respond by holding onto his position more tightly and trying to justify it in a confrontational dynamic. Consider this instead:

> *"I feel that your asking price is too high."*

This is my opinion. It is how I feel. We are all entitled to our own feelings and opinions. If I can offer a reason in support, it is even better. In any event, it is non-judgmental and non-confrontational. We can carry on negotiating without any bad feelings.

In addition to using I rather than you, these examples emphasize feelings and perceptions. Your counterpart may not share your feelings or perceptions, but he can hardly fault you for them. Here are some more guidelines to remember:

- **Avoid using words that suggest the other party is to blame or is wrong.** Do not criticize, judge, or find fault. This will only put your counterpart on the defensive. Instead, emphasize your feelings and perceptions. For example, compare:

"Don't rush me!"

This suggests that the other party is unfairly pressuring me. It suggests that I am judging him. He may resent the implication.

"I'd like some time to think about it."

This expresses my feelings without regard to the other party's motives. It cannot cause offense.

- **Describe rather than judge.** An objective description of fact may be disputed, but its mere form will not offend the way a judgment will. For example:

"Your offer is unreasonably low."

Your counterpart may be offended by this judgment on your part. You are saying he is unreasonable.

"I feel your offer of a three per cent increase is inadequate in light of current industry trends."

This statement is more specific, descriptive, and verifiable, even if "current industry trends" is debatable. It is non-judgmental and unlikely to cause offense.

- **The words we use in a negotiation greatly affect its emotional climate.** Avoid negative words, value-laden words and emotional or hot button words. Use positive, collaborative, and constructive words.

COMMON EMOTIONS IN NEGOTIATION

Humans experience many feelings and emotions, most of which have little impact on a negotiation. The two that are most likely to derail a negotiation are anger and fear.

Anger

Anger is widely thought to be an ugly emotion, a monster that pops out in stressful situations to urge us on to intimidate, punish, and exact revenge. Anger is the most difficult emotion to control. While it may seem appropriate to display anger at the time, in retrospect it rarely is, and we usually regret it afterwards.

We often express anger in an attempt to intimidate the other party, thereby giving us some measure of control over them. This is easy to understand when we are focused on winning, getting our way, or proving ourselves to be "right." We must appear strong and in control. Anger lets us do this.

However, there is another way to look at anger. It serves to protect us against some perceived threat to our well-being or self-esteem. As anger is a protective emotion, when we feel anger we must ask what we are protecting ourselves against. We perceive a threat. What is the threat? It is often the result of frustration, the threat of not getting what we want and the need to protect our ego. Similarly, when we see another person expressing anger, we must remember that he feels threatened. What is he threatened by? What is he trying to protect?

Anger is often seen as a sign of strength. In fact, anger is often a sign of weakness or an attempt to protect against vulnerability. True strength consists of controlling our anger, and channeling it in an appropriate manner. While it may be natural to feel anger, a win-win negotiator will react to it constructively. Unless anger is managed, it can derail a negotiation—and a relationship.

The general rule is: don't express your anger. Of course, there are exceptions. If you do express anger, do so because you *choose to act angry* when justified. For example, a hard-nosed negotiator may provoke you to test your response. While remaining calm and in control is normally the best response, you may decide that a controlled release of anger or a display of righteous indignation will show your counterpart that you are not a pushover. Mr Tough Guy might interpret this as a show of strength and respect you more for it. Once you've proved your mettle, he won't mess with you again.

Some negotiators will unleash an outburst of anger in the hope of squeezing a concession from their counterpart. The ploy may succeed, but it will breed resentment, and you may pay the price for it later. You can get a concession without stooping to such low tactics.

Suppose your counterpart is not a win-win negotiator. Suppose he cannot control his emotions, or uses his anger as a club. How should you respond? Here are my suggestions:

- First of all, you must allow his anger to run its course. You cannot reason with someone in an emotionally charged state, so don't even try. Stop the discussion. Let him vent. This would be a good time to take a break. Use this time to try to understand the reason behind the anger. Resume negotiating only after his anger has dissipated.

- Just because a person has calmed down, do not assume he is no longer angry. Chances are the issues underlying the anger are still there. You must address these concerns, but only after the emotional storm has passed.

- Ask the magic question: "Did I do anything to upset you?" If she says yes, find out what it is and deal with it. If she says no, she will probably recognize that she is dumping on you unfairly and calm down.

- Accept his anger as valid. While expressing anger is not always appropriate, your counterpart has a right to his feelings. Empathize. You might say:

  "I see you are angry. You obviously feel strongly about this, and I'd like to understand why this is so important to you."

  Encourage him to share his thoughts, and listen attentively.

- Maintain your own composure in the face of an angry outburst from your counterpart. Do not fight fire with fire—you'll only get a bigger fire!

- Do not take it personally. Your counterpart may be angry with himself, frustrated with the situation, or trying to mask his own weakness or insecurity. Do not assume you are the target, because chances are you are not.

- Do not appease your counterpart by offering a concession. Make a concession only in exchange for a concession from your counterpart, and only at a point when reason prevails. Once you give something up to buy approval from the other party, guess what you'll get? More outbursts! And why not—your counterpart will have discovered a successful strategy for negotiating with you.

- Apologize when warranted, or even when it's not. An apology costs nothing, and it makes the other party feel better. Don't let pride stand in the way of satisfying your interests.

- Focus on the big picture. Remember that you are not negotiating to prove that you are right or to serve your ego; you are negotiating to satisfy your interests and improve your position.

I went through law school driving a series of clunkers. By my final year, I had had enough of breakdowns and expensive repairs and decided it was time to buy my first new car. After all, I would be a lawyer soon and would be able to pay for it, so why wait? I did my research and decided on an entry-level Volkswagen that had excellent reviews. I also came up with a negotiating strategy: I would tell the salesman that I was not going to trade in my old car, and then after negotiating the best deal possible, I would change my mind and ask how much I could get for my worthless heap. This lawyer-to-be (who had never bought a new car before) was going to teach the unsuspecting salesman (who sold cars every day for a living) a few things about negotiation! After negotiating what seemed like the best deal possible, I sprung my little surprise. The salesman went ballistic! He ranted about how he had been negotiating in good faith and I pulled this [expletive] on him ... unethical ... [more expletives] ... *yadda, yadda, yadda* ... I knew it was all an act, he was a big boy, he had seen this all before, he wasn't really angry, he just wanted to use the emotional sledgehammer to intimidate me into agreeing to the deal he wanted. I didn't cave in, or appreciate his manner of customer relations. Which is why my first new car was a Subaru.

Fear

There are four basic types of fear: fear of the unknown, fear of loss, fear of failure, and fear of rejection. They all have implications for negotiators, so you should understand how they affect you and your counterpart and be prepared to deal with them.

Fear of the unknown

People fear what they do not know or understand. A negotiation may have high stakes and an uncertain outcome; even the process may be unfamiliar and inspire fear.

The antidote to this is preparation. Learn as much as you can about your interests and currencies, as well as those of your counterpart. Develop a strong Plan B. Gather information about the subject matter and context of the negotiation. Get comfortable with the process. Preparation leads to confidence, and confidence helps you to manage fear.

Fear of loss

No one likes to lose, but some people have a strong aversion to risk. In fact, most people are more strongly motivated by a fear of loss than they are by the prospect of gain. Their fear of losing money or paying too much can cause them to miss out on a good opportunity. Conversely, their fear of missing out on an opportunity can cause them to make a bad deal.

Preparation also helps to combat fear of loss. Before you begin bargaining, know your bottom line and your Plan B, and stick to them. Be prepared to walk away. You may reassess these in light of new information and changing situations, but do so with the same sobriety that went into your pre-negotiation assessment.

In addition, understand that a calculated risk is not the same as a foolish risk. There is always some element of risk in a negotiation. However, if you allow yourself to become paralyzed with fear, you will not negotiate much, nor will you gain much. Remember that negotiation has elements of skill and chance, and the more skillful you are at preparing, the less you will be affected by chance.

Fear of failure

While fear of loss and fear of failure often go together, fear of loss relates to tangibles (money, opportunity) while fear of failure relates to intangible losses, such as damage to pride, ego, or reputation, or embarrassment or loss of face. These emotional losses may be harder to bear than monetary losses.

The very prospect of losing face can cause a negotiator to ignore his best interests and embrace a losing cause. As he doesn't want to admit he was wrong, he continues to pursue a doomed strategy in the irrational hope that things will turn out well. This escalation of commitment strikes even seasoned negotiators. Guard against it with thorough pre-negotiation preparation and by asking team members for reality checks during the negotiation.

A win-win mindset can offset fear of failure, as well as fear of losing and fear of the unknown. Approaching a negotiation as a chance to solve a problem collaboratively with your counterpart minimizes fear of failing or losing as the focus is on getting a win for both parties. The emphasis on asking questions, listening, and empathizing builds trust and sheds light on the unknown. The spirit of exploring options and creating value keeps the discussion positive as fear takes a back seat.

Fear of rejection

A special fear of failure is fear of rejection. We don't like to hear the word no. Most people, upon hearing the word no, get discouraged and give up. They equate rejection of their request as a personal rejection. They are afraid to pursue the matter for fear they may be seen as overbearing. Sometimes they just don't want to risk further rejection.

To overcome this fear of rejection, remind yourself that your idea has been rejected, perhaps because your counterpart doesn't understand your request. Follow up with a "why not?" to understand her thinking. Make sure she understands you.

The word no is rarely final. Whenever you hear a no, treat it as an opening position—an invitation to negotiate. Modify your proposal and consider other options. Try to turn that no into a yes.

While no is usually seen as a rejection, it is better thought of as an opportunity. Recall the discussion of how to handle a no in Chapter 5.

The key to overcoming these fears is preparation—a major theme that I've been emphasizing throughout this book. In addition, remember these tips:

- **Do not appear too eager for a deal.** Once you demonstrate an emotional desire for the subject of the negotiation, your counterpart will be able to deal with you on his terms.

- **Have a strong Plan B.** This gives you confidence and guarantees you will not be worse off after the negotiation than you were before.

- **Be prepared to walk away.** Making a bad deal is worse than making no deal at all.

- **Do not show fear.** Wear your poker face. Remember that much of negotiating power is based largely on perception. It's important to appear confident and in control.

Bear in mind that your negotiating counterpart, being human, also experiences these fears to some degree. How much will depend on his perceptions, level of confidence, preparation, and strength of will.

One common piece of advice on dealing with fear generally is to tell yourself you are not afraid. This is bad advice! Your body feels the fear and knows you are lying! Instead of trying to deny your fear, reframe it as excitement. Excitement feels like fear, but is positive.

For example, many people love to ride roller coasters. They scream in terror for the entire ride, and then say "That was fun! Let's do it again!" They label their feeling as excitement instead of fear. If you think you feel fear when contemplating a negotiation, try telling yourself it's exciting.

PERSONAL ATTACKS

Negotiations can get intense. Long hours, incompatible demands, unmet expectations, personality and cultural clashes, and lack of progress can frustrate the participants. Tempers rise. Harsh words are exchanged. Things can get personal.

It is natural to defend yourself when attacked, and maybe even launch a counterattack against the other side. These attacks and counterattacks can spiral out of control and cause emotions to flare and egos to bruise. They make an agreement less likely.

The best negotiators do not launch personal attacks, nor do they respond to such attacks in kind. If you do find yourself in an emotionally charged spiral of escalating attacks, try to defuse it. The simple act of apologizing can do wonders. An apology followed by a question shows concern for the other party and allows him the opportunity to be heard. For example:

"I'm sorry, I didn't mean to seem unreasonable. Is there anything else you would like to add?"

And don't forget the magic question discussed earlier: "Did I say anything to upset you?" If they say yes, apologize and deal with it; if they say no they will have little choice but to calm down.

HARSH OR CONDESCENDING COMMENTS

It never pays to use harsh, bitter, sarcastic, or belittling comments during a negotiation. This makes you look unprofessional at best and unhinged at worst. You might think that provoking your counterpart might be a good strategy, the way Tom Cruise's prosecutor character did with Jack Nicholson's Marine Colonel Jessup in *A Few Good Men* ("You can't handle the truth!"), but a negotiation isn't a trial or a movie. There is always a better way to get what you want without rolling in the gutter, ruining a relationship, and building resentment towards you.

In addition, do not make patronizing or value-laden comments about how fair you are being to your counterpart. Suggesting the other party would be unreasonable not to agree with you is alienating. For example, a seemingly reassuring comment such as "I believe you will find our offer to be most generous" sounds like a perfectly reasonable way to encourage the other party to accept your offer. However, the other party is likely to interpret it like this: *"I'm doing you a huge favor and you'd be a fool to reject it!"*

Think about the ways in which your counterpart can take your comments. Do not use language that may be insulting, such as:

- "That's ridiculous!"
- "Are you out of your mind?"
- "Don't be such a cheapskate."

Needless to say, you must avoid obscenity, ethnic slurs, and other offensive language.

MANAGING EXPECTATIONS—KEEPING THEM HAPPY

Perception is a big part of negotiating. It isn't always whether you win or lose that matters, it's whether you *feel* you've won or lost. The subjective outcome is more important than any objective measure of the outcome. People need to feel good about the process and the outcome, regardless of how well they actually fare substantively. We have to meet expectations.

In addition, the negotiation process must appear to be fair. People have a powerfully strong sense of fairness—it's hard-wired into our brains. If you or the process seems unfair, your counterpart will resent you and your relationship will suffer.

A popular activity in negotiation classes illustrates the point. Students are paired up, and one student (the offeror) is given $100 to share with his partner (the offeree) according to an allocation dictated by the offeror. However, the offeree has the right to accept the offer and share the money according to the proposed allocation, or reject it, in which case no one gets any money. A 50:50 offer is invariably accepted. Often the offeror will feel entitled to a larger share and offer a 60:40 split, or a 75:25 split. Some of these will be accepted, but the more unequal the proposed split, the more likely it is that the offeree will play the spoiler and reject the offer. A truly rational person would accept an extreme offer of even $1, as he would still be better off monetarily—$1 is better than nothing. But people aren't rational—they are emotional, and they have a strong sense of fairness. They may choose a lose-lose outcome rather than stand for what they perceive to be unfair treatment.

People can be extremely emotional and irrational when they feel they are not being treated fairly or with due respect. Take pains to be fair and respectful throughout the negotiation. Make sure the negotiation process itself is also fair and impartial.

BIASES

Irrationality may also take the form of biases. Even when our emotions are in check, our thinking processes are often corrupted by biases we are not even aware of. Psychologists have catalogued them by the dozens; a quick scan on Wikipedia turns up almost two hundred. Some of them are mental shortcuts that help us cope with a complex world, but they can get us into trouble. It pays to be on guard against them. Here are some of the more relevant ones for negotiators to watch out for.

Stereotyping

Stereotyping refers to the politically incorrect but still human tendency to assume certain attributes in another based on their membership in a demographic group. The group can be defined by race, religion, gender, culture, occupation, etc. We often resort to stereotyping as a way of getting to "know" more about our counterpart in a shorter period of time. The problem is (aside from political correctness!) twofold: people belong to multiple groups, and people are also individuals.

Don't play in to the stereotyping trap. Evaluate each person as the unique individual he is.

Selective perception

We see what we're looking for and ignore information that doesn't support our beliefs. This bias can be very costly in many areas of life, whether negotiating, considering investment options, or choosing a mate. Selective perception can magnify the effects of stereotypes ("I knew he would do that, it's so typical

of his kind!") and the halo effect ("She's smart, beautiful, witty—
perfect in every way!).

To counteract the bias of selective perception, make it a point
to play the devil's advocate. Get a reality check from friends or
colleagues. Actively seek information contrary to your initial
assessment or preferred outcome.

Projection

Projection refers to our tendency to see in others what we see
or feel in ourselves. We often assume others think, feel, and
behave like us. If we like something, they will like it too. (And
if we don't trust someone, maybe it's a sign that we are not
so trustworthy ourselves!) This can cause us to misunderstand
our counterpart's intentions. It can also cause us to miss
opportunities if we assume our counterpart values something
the same way we do. For example, we may value the money,
while they may be more motivated by relationship, ego, or
some other consideration.

You can help counteract projection by assessing your counterpart
objectively and trying to understand her wants and motivations
as an individual. Using MESOs[*] is a good way to zero in on what
your counterpart values most.

Mythical fixed-pie

The win-lose, law of the jungle model of negotiating is hard-

---

[*] Multiple Equivalent Simultaneous Offers, discussed in Chapter 3.

wired into many people, who just can't accept the notion of win-win, integrative negotiating. Those who have this view assume all negotiations are distributive, and any gain enjoyed by their counterpart must come at their own expense. It's all about trying to grab the biggest piece of the pie, rather than exploring ways to make the pie bigger for all parties. Old habits die hard, and it may take some time and practice to learn to see things from the principled negotiation perspective.

Be patient as you begin to implement win-win negotiating techniques into your repertoire. Focus on interests, identifying currencies and options, creating value, and the joint problem solving approach. The checklist at the end of this book can be a big help in adopting the win-win framework.

Availability of information

Gathering information takes time and effort, so we rely more on what is readily available. Easily recalled information is not only used more, but may be perceived as more accurate than it actually is simply by virtue of its salience. As a result, the source of the information can have an undue influence on our thinking.

How can you reduce the impact of the availability bias? Question the accuracy and source of the information you encounter. Be especially aware of colorful language and imagery. Is it being used to influence you? Seek out contrary information from other sources and evaluate it objectively.

Law of small numbers

This bias is a form of information availability. Based on a small number of incidents, you make a broad generalization that may be incorrect. For example, surveys based on a small number of responses are suspect because the pool of information may not reflect the wider population.

This danger of erroneous extrapolation from a limited information set applies in many areas of life. Let's say you buy a Toyonda sports coupe. It breaks down every few weeks. Your friend also buys one and has a similarly awful experience. Does that mean all Toyonda cars are lousy? You can't reach that conclusion based on two instances. Maybe Toyonda was voted Car of the Year, and the one you got was an outlier.

By now you may have noticed a pattern in the ways to protect yourself against these biases: be aware, do your homework, and get a reality check.

Winner's curse

Everyone likes to get what they want, but when we get what we want too easily, we may have a nagging concern that we could have done better. We wonder why our counterpart agreed so readily and didn't put up more of a fight. This is the winner's curse, a form of buyer's remorse. It is especially common in auctions, where the bidders are caught up in the excitement and the winner wonders whether he paid too much. The winner thinks to himself: no one else was willing to pay that much—did I overpay? We also see this in the realm of business acquisitions, where the acquiring company pays a premium that more often than not turns out to have been excessive.

The best way to avoid this form of regret is to prepare thoroughly. Make an accurate assessment of the subject of the negotiation, so that you are confident about what a fair price is. Approach the negotiation soberly, understanding and protecting yourself against emotional considerations. You might also negotiate a contingent agreement or guarantee that will allow for an adjustment if things do not turn out as expected. For example, if you are buying a business based on certain representations such as sales projections, you could agree to adjust the final price depending on what the actual numbers prove to be at a future date.

Self-serving biases

In evaluating others, we tend to overstate the role of personal factors over situational ones. We blame our own shortcomings on the situation—it's never our fault! If you are late for an appointment, it's because traffic was a mess. If the other guy is late, it's because he is irresponsible!

We tend to have certain biases in the way we apportion credit and blame. When things turn out favorably for us, we are likely to attribute the results to our own ability. We think "*I achieved a good result because I worked hard, I prepared well, I am a great negotiator, I deserve it.*" When we don't do so well, we find external reasons to explain the result: "*They got lucky, they deceived me, the economy worked against me, there was nothing I could do about it.*" Or we may discount the effects of external or situational factors and assume our counterpart has more skill, expertise, or ability than he really does.

We may think things will turn out better for us than for others. *"That could never happen to me; it only happens to other people."* Then again, some people think they always get the lemons in life, and everyone else has it better.

Many people think more highly of themselves than of others: *"I am smarter, more skillful, more honest, more open minded, and fairer than him. He is so rigid, irrational, and biased."* Your counterpart probably thinks the same about you! How a particular individual actually interprets these things depends on a host of psychological factors, such as self-esteem, locus of control, and others beyond the scope of this book. Just be aware that we are all subject to these biases and try to understand and minimize the effect they have on you.

An effective negotiator tries to be objective and open to possibilities. She will still be biased, but she will be more willing to accept that she has faults and makes mistakes, and tries to correct for them. When you take responsibility for your shortcomings, you have an opportunity to learn from your mistakes and do better next time.

Endowment effect

In one of my favorite psychology experiments, researchers gave half the members of a group a free gift (coffee mugs, pens, and other items). The lucky recipients were asked to write down how much they would sell their gift for. The ones who didn't receive the gift were asked to write down how much they would be willing to pay for the item. On average, those who had the gift valued it two to three times more than those who did not receive the gift. A few minutes before, when no one had received the gift, the average value assigned by the group would have been somewhere in between these two figures. The mere fact of possessing something leads those who have it to value it more than the market does. Psychologists call this the "endowment effect."

Due to the endowment effect, we tend to overvalue what's ours and undervalue what belongs to others. This often prevents us from recognizing a good deal when it's right in front of us. It also blinds us to realities.

Let's say you are putting your house up for sale. You will probably ask for more than it's worth just because it's your house. "*Ah, the memories! That's where my daughter took her first step!*" Of course you value it highly, but the market doesn't care about these sentimental considerations, it's just a house, worth no more or less than any similar house. If you list it for too much, no one will make an offer. After a while, you realize your mistake and lower the price. The bargain hunters take note, sense desperation, and bombard you with lowball offers. Good luck getting a deal now. It would have turned out better if you had priced it more realistically in the first place.

Once again, the prescription is to be aware of the bias, prepare well, and get a reality check by isolating sentimentality and understanding how the market perceives your situation.

Reactive devaluation

Reactive devaluation is a cousin of the endowment effect. We minimize the value of the other party's ideas, proposals, or concessions simply because it came from them. This is a classic adversarial, win-lose behavior: we are suspicious of what they offer because we believe they are more concerned with their interests than with ours. There is some truth to this, but that doesn't mean our counterpart can't have an idea that serves us better than our own idea.

Look critically at what your counterpart advocates, but keep an open mind and try to see the benefits. Be objective, not dismissive. Weigh the pros and cons of every idea without regard to who proposed it. Ask the opinion of a colleague or impartial third party who does not have a stake in the outcome.

A good negotiator recognizes that he and his counterpart both have these biases. He strives to accept the other party as an equal. He understands that by thinking ill of his counterpart, their trust and communication will suffer, as will the likelihood of reaching a win-win outcome.

Overconfidence

Confidence is a double-edged sword. A healthy dose of confidence—especially when it's the result of solid preparation—is valued in the business world and is an asset to any negotiator. In addition, research has proven that negotiators with higher aspirations going into a negotiation tend to emerge with better outcomes. It's a form of self-fulfilling prophecy.

On the other hand, overconfidence is dangerous. If you think you have everything all figured out, you are less likely to ask questions, test assumptions, and make a realistic assessment of the situation. Overconfidence can blind you to new information and other options that may have a bearing on the outcome. Be prepared to change your assumptions, strategy, and even your expectations in light of new developments.

The line between confidence and overconfidence is often murky. In American politics, voters like confidence and punish inconsistency. Pity the poor politician who has been branded a waffler or flip-flopper by his opponent. That label is often the kiss of death. Never mind that times change and positions evolve—a candidate who sticks to his guns will be seen more favorably than one who tries to explain why she changed. So it's easy to see why confidence, conviction, and certainty are so highly admired, even at the risk of being overconfident.

It's good to be confident, but not *too* confident. To guard against overconfidence and the mistakes that follow, try to understand all the elements in play, make a realistic assessment of the situation, and always watch for new information. A famous quote (attributed to various statesmen and economists) is good advice: "When the facts change, I change my mind." So do the best negotiators.

Argument dilution

Most negotiators offer as many arguments as they can think of to support their position. They think that the more arguments they have, the stronger their cause. In fact, advancing too many arguments dilutes the strength of your main point.

It is better to have one or two strong points in support of your argument than a whole slew of them. When a mix of stronger and weaker arguments is presented, the weaker or less relevant information dilutes the impact of the stronger or more relevant information. If you try to overwhelm your counterpart with an avalanche of points, she will probably focus on the weakest link and dismiss all of the others with it. Don't make it easy for her to refute you. Focus on your best couple of reasons and forget about the less convincing ones. It's about quality, not quantity.

Losing focus

Having invested time, money, effort, and ego into a negotiation, you may feel pressure to reach an agreement, even if it is not to your advantage. You may feel that all you have invested will be wasted if you don't come away with a deal. These outlays are not true investments, they are sunk costs. Whatever you have put into the negotiation is gone. At this point, your task is to decide whether you will be better off with the deal than without it. No deal is better than a bad deal. Focus on your objective, not on what you have already "lost."

People often act on impulse. At times you may be distracted by shiny baubles that are appealing but are not among your negotiating priorities. How many people have ever bought a cosmetic product just to get the "free gift" that comes with it? Or a candy bar they didn't know they wanted until they saw it while waiting in the checkout lane? Keep your impulses in check and focus on what you're negotiating for.

It is never too late to walk away. Focus on your interests, remember your Plan B, and remain cordial. You may be able to resume negotiations later.

A win-win negotiator recognizes his own emotions and biases, and he takes steps to compensate for them. He also pays attention to the emotions and biases of his negotiating partner. Some of these can be used tactically, as when the Volkswagen salesman used an emotional outburst in an attempt to get me to cave in. There are many other tactics beyond emotional outbursts. As we will see in the next chapter, the win-win negotiator understands a wide range of negotiating tactics and is able to respond with the appropriate counter-tactic.

CHAPTER 7

NEGOTIATING TACTICS AND COUNTER-TACTICS

*"When the only tool you have is a hammer,
every problem begins to resemble a nail."*
—Abraham Maslow

Negotiation is a game, and as in most games, there are many different tactics and counter-tactics. Tactics—the plays, the parries and thrusts—are a part of nearly every negotiation. For every tactic (offensive maneuver) there is a counter-tactic, or defense. If you want to be a great negotiator, you will need to be familiar with a wide range of tactics, and you must also know how to defend against them with an appropriate counter-tactic. You need to be able to juggle them around and choose the best ones for any given situation.

WHY DO WE NEED TACTICS?

We have discussed a number of reasons why win-win negotiation, or "principled negotiation," is the way of the future. Business today values long-term relationships rather than one-off, win-lose contests. There is a need for collaboration, even among competitors. We see more joint ventures, co-branding arrangements, and strategic partnerships. The law of the jungle is no longer the norm.

Some of the hallmarks of win-win negotiating are joint problem solving, effective communication, trust, fairness, and maintaining healthy and mutually rewarding long-term relationships. The relationship issue is key here because we are, in essence, negotiating with partners rather than adversaries.

With all of these high-minded ideals, you may be wondering, "Why bother with tactics? Aren't tactics just a bunch of dirty tricks?" Sometimes they are, sometimes they're not, and sometimes it depends.

Have you ever noticed that, in a bargaining situation, sellers tend to ask for a higher price than they are willing to accept? And that a buyer's first offer is usually less than he is willing to pay? It's a classic example of the old dictum "Buy low and sell high." This highball and lowball opening gambit is one of the most frequently used negotiating tactics.

As this simple tactic is so common, we almost expect to encounter it whenever we bargain. In fact, we would find it hard to believe that an opening bid could be anyone's true bottom line. Consequently, when we hear the opening price stated, we naturally begin to bargain. No doubt our counterpart would respond in the same way.

Remember, negotiation is a game. Some tactics are expected, even between such intimate negotiating partners as husbands and wives. We are expected to use certain tactics as part of the game.

There is another reason why you need tactics and counter-tactics. You are learning how to become a win-win negotiator. However, your counterpart may be an old-school, adversarial negotiator. She may use tactics against you, so it's important that you are able to recognize and counter them.

Finally, there may be times when you *want* to use tactics. In a one-off, distributive negotiation (such as buying a used car), you may not be concerned about how the other party fares. You may choose to use tactics to get the best deal for yourself.

Negotiation tactics are not always black and white, fair or unfair, ethical or unethical. There is a lot of gray. You need to be prepared for whatever may come your way.

INITIAL OFFERS AND COUNTER-OFFERS

As we've just seen, most negotiations involve a dance around high and low opening offers and counter-offers. If you want to dance, you need to learn the steps.

No one expects a first offer to be the best offer. This is one reason why you should never accept an opening offer. You know your counterpart is highballing or lowballing. You know you can negotiate for a better offer, and it would be foolish not to.

But there is another reason you should not accept a first offer: it would make the other person feel like he has been taken advantage of.

If you're wondering why, imagine you are at a neighbor's yard sale and see a wonderful antique cabinet. You ask the owner how much, and he replies $200. Immediately, you say "I'll take it!" and whip out your wallet. The seller would have been willing to accept less after a little give and take bargaining. When you quickly agreed to his first highball offer, he was surprised. Now, he feels that you must know something that he doesn't and you've gotten a fantastic deal, and he is a sucker. Even though you accepted his price, he feels like he is on the losing end of a win-lose transaction. He expected to play the game, his expectations were not met, and he is dissatisfied. Your neighbor would probably resent you, and the bad feeling could impact any future relationship.

On the other hand, suppose you had counter-offered $150, and after a bit of bargaining, ultimately agreed on $175. You would have gotten a better deal, and the seller would feel that he got a fair price. His expectations of haggling and meeting in the middle would have been satisfied, and he would be happy. Never accept the first offer. Even if you are delighted with the first offer, make an effort to haggle. Your counterpart will feel better.

WHO GOES FIRST?

The opening offer and counter-offer dynamic is simple to understand. More complicated is the question of *who* should make the opening offer.

Some people feel it is better to open the negotiation themselves. Others advocate never making the first move. Which is correct? It depends! There is evidence in support of both positions. Let's consider each approach.

Approach #1: Let the other party make the initial offer whenever possible

You might be pleasantly surprised. Your counterpart's initial offer might be more favorable than you expected. It might be better than anything you would have dared to ask for. If so, good for you, but remember, don't accept a first offer immediately. Haggle a bit so your counterpart feels like a winner. People are more satisfied when they work for it.

You learn something. Regardless of whether the first offer is high or low, it tells you something about your counterpart's mindset, aspirations, confidence, and perhaps his sense of reality. It gives you a bit more information about him before you begin bargaining.

If his initial offer is not favorable, you can start bargaining. If you do not like his first offer (or even if you do), you can always make a counter-offer and begin bargaining. You have nothing to lose by listening, as long as you heed the next paragraph.

If the initial offer is way out of line, dismiss it firmly but politely. Do not respond to an unrealistic offer. Flinch (see page 193) and explain that you really cannot respond to such an offer, then wait for something more reasonable. Once you make a counter-offer, you have in effect legitimized his initial offer, which becomes an anchor point for the entire negotiation. That first offer, combined with your counter-offer, establishes a negotiating range. Chances are that any agreement will be somewhere near the middle of that range, and how favorable that middle figure turns out to be will depend on the first figure from your counterpart that you respond to.

As you can see, there is ample support for letting the other party make the initial offer. Let's consider the alternative.

Approach #2: Make the initial offer yourself

The initial offer is a powerful anchor. It establishes one end of the negotiating range, and thus affects the settlement price. It is to your advantage to set the initial anchor point yourself, rather than allow your counterpart to do so.

Your initial offer should be at the high end of your aspiration range, and within or close to your counterpart's acceptable range. As you will probably have to make concessions anyway, it's best to start from a high figure and make your counterpart work for any concessions. Don't give anything away before you begin bargaining.

However, you don't want to start out too high. Try to set a high anchor, but a realistic one. If you set it too high, you could lose credibility, and your counterpart will resent you. Make sure your initial offer is attractive to you and something your counterpart could conceivably accept.

Use an odd number. Exact figures look as if they were calculated according to a precise mathematical formula and have an aura of permanence about them. It is harder to dispute an odd number than a nice round figure that looks as if it were made up without any thought.

Imagine a salesman saying "$10,000 is my absolute bottom line." Would you believe him? Probably not. You'd wonder why not $9,999.95 or $9,990? If he had said "I can't go a cent below $9,987.64", you might think he had sharpened his pencil as much as possible, and you would probably accept the figure without question.

Support your offer with reasons, but invite and be open to their counter-proposal. Once you have presented your initial offer—an odd figure from the high end of your aspiration range—in writing, explain why that figure (which probably seems high to your counterpart) is fair. Ask him what he thinks, and listen attentively. Wait for his counter-offer and carry on from there. Just remember that if his initial counter-offer is unrealistic, do not allow it to take hold as an anchor point.

There are certain situations where it is especially advantageous for you to make the first offer. If it is a complicated negotiation with many elements other than price, your proposal becomes the benchmark. Your counterpart may use your proposal as the basis for future discussion, or as a reference for comparison with his own ideas. Your offer sets the tone for the negotiations that follow.

If you are the seller and think you know more about the subject of the negotiation, make the first offer and set an aggressive anchor. However, if it's a unique item (a fine painting or antique rather than a five-year-old Toyonda), you may not want to name a price in the hope that a very interested buyer will make a high offer. The range of likely bids for a unique item is wide, and a determined buyer might just make an offer beyond your wildest expectations. We often hear of paintings by top tier artists being sold at auctions at prices way beyond the experts' estimates. However, a five-year-old Toyonda is just a commodity and a buyer is not likely to pay a premium for it.

If you are the buyer and think you know more about the item's value, let the seller name a price. Hope for a pleasant surprise but be prepared for anything, and always have a Plan B.

If you are the buyer (or seller for that matter) and don't have a good idea of the item's value, you are not ready to negotiate! Do your homework first.

ANCHORS

The first offer in a negotiation and the ensuing counter-offer serve as anchor points. These anchor points establish the settlement range, as the price you ultimately agree to will be somewhere in between those points. These anchors are references that we use to make comparisons that guide our decisions about whether to accept an offer or what counter-offer to make.

Other references also serve as anchors. The list price of an item at retail is perhaps the best known example of an anchor. Have you ever been impressed with an item's "sale" price as compared with its regular price? Taken on its own, a sale price may not be attractive by any objective standard, but when compared with a higher figure it looks more appealing.

A list price, a bid price, the price of a similar item, or a previous price for a similar or identical item can also be seen as anchors. In non-price negotiations, a previous instance or precedent can serve as a standard of comparison. An anchor draws us to a figure—often arbitrary—and makes the eventual settlement price appear more attractive by comparison.

We use references and comparisons as short cuts. Short cuts are intended to save time and make our life easier, but they can be dangerous. By relying on an anchor point, we suspend our objectivity. We rely on anchor points all the time, even if they have no basis in reality. A number thrown out at random, completely unrelated to the subject of the negotiation, can affect the settlement price in the negotiation. And while you may make some correction when evaluating anchors ("I know he's trying to highball me, let me compensate by making a lowball counter-offer …"), it is not usually enough to overcome the anchoring effect.

The important thing is to understand how anchor points work, and be vigilant against their effects. This example may help.

Imagine you are on holiday on some exotic tropical island. A local approaches you in the market with a string of beads made by the natives. "Good morning, sir. Would you like to buy this beautiful necklace? The usual price is $30, but for you, only $15." You might think you're getting a huge discount and take it. Or you might remember that you should never accept a first offer, and make a counter-offer of $10. In that case, you may end up buying the necklace for about $12 or $13. Or you might counter-offer $5, in which case you would probably end up paying about $10 if you decide to buy it. If the initial pitch had been "Usual price is $30, but for you, only $20," you would have paid more, depending on your counter-offer. The price you ultimately agree on is a function of the range set by the anchor points.

	Scenario A	Scenario B	Scenario C	Scenario D
First offer	$15	$15	$20	$20
Counter-offer	$5	$10	$10	$15
Settlement	$10	$12–13	$15	$17–18

Based on the four scenarios above, we see that the buyer is better off when the range is lower, that is, when the seller's first offer is lower, or when his own counter-offer is lower, or both. The buyer should not respond to a high first offer from the seller; instead, he should try to get the seller to make a lower offer before making his counter-offer, thus avoiding the high anchor. The buyer should also make a lower counter-offer than he would otherwise be comfortable making, which would also tend to result in a lower settlement price. This is all intuitive, but easier said than done. Many buyers are easily led by a high anchor, and are reluctant to make a lowball counter-offer. They might be worried that their counterpart will perceive them as stingy, or they might be uncomfortable bargaining hard. However, if you can push yourself beyond your comfort zone, you will capture more value in all of your future negotiations.

Similarly, the seller is better off when she makes a higher first offer, rejects a lowball counter-offer, or both, as this will raise the settlement range. Many sellers are uncomfortable doing this.

They may be afraid that the buyer will think they are greedy or unreasonable. Or they may not believe that their product or service is worth much, and so they ask for less. But if the seller can get comfortable with a more aggressive first offer, she will make more money in her subsequent negotiations.

Our discussion of initial offers, counter-offers, and anchor points yields a few rules:

- As part of your preparation, know where the range of reasonable lies and what is extreme.
- Always ask for more than you expect to get.
- Always offer less than you think the other party will accept.
- Never accept the first offer.
- Be aware of the anchoring effect and how anchors determine the negotiating range and influence the settlement price.
- Don't let your counterpart set an unrealistic anchor. If his offer is too extreme, don't make a counter-offer.
- If your counterpart feels your offer is too ambitious, don't concede—justify your offer.
- Be more ambitious when making your first offer or counter-offer. Go as far as you can without crossing the line between reasonable and extreme.

CONCESSIONS

Almost every negotiation requires concessions before you can reach an agreement. Like so much of negotiating, making and receiving concessions is natural and intuitive. The danger comes when we think we already know it all and miss out on the nuances that can make a difference in many of our negotiations.

A concession is when you moderate your position to move closer to your counterpart. For example, raising the amount of your offer, lowering your asking price, forgoing a demand, or offering other value to your counterpart are all forms of concession. The way you pattern your concessions will send important signals to your counterpart and influence his responses. It is important that you make concessions the right way to avoid being eaten alive.

My daughter Cherisse grew up in Asia, where the Chinese New Year is a major holiday. Part of the celebration involves visiting relatives, who always have a wide array of snacks on hand. One popular treat is chocolate "coins" wrapped in gold foil, which comes in two sizes. During one such visit when Cherisse was about two years old, she spied the coins (and somehow knew there was chocolate inside) and said, "Daddy, I want two big coins."

I replied, "You cannot have two big coins."

"One big and one small."

"You cannot have two coins."

"One big one then!"

The little pixie negotiator already knew how to pattern her concessions, without having been taught by anyone! She conceded as little as possible to maximize her outcome.

Suppose you are a buyer negotiating to purchase an item. You are prepared to pay up to $1,000 more than your initial offer. How should you pattern your concessions?

First of all, don't offer a concession right away. If you appear too willing to give concessions, your negotiating partner will assume you will give more as the negotiation progresses. Make your partner work for it. The harder he works, the more he values the result.

Secondly, label your concessions. Make it clear with each concession that you are giving up something of value that requires reciprocation. Do not allow your concessions to be dismissed as minor. If you do not seem to be giving up much when conceding, the other party may not think much of it either. Value is largely subjective, so encourage the perception of value.

Thirdly, do not offer a large portion of your $1,000 at once. That also signals that more concessions are on the way. Start with a modest concession, with later concessions of diminishing size. By making your concessions smaller, less frequent, and less easily given, you are signaling to your counterpart that you are approaching your bottom line.

Another reason that supports breaking up concessions into smaller pieces comes from research. Most people prefer to receive bad news all at once, like ripping off a bandage. But we derive more appreciation from receiving good news in multiple installments rather than all at once.* This suggests that the same

---

* From the work of Amos Tversky and Daniel Kahneman, discussed in Deepak Malhotra, "Four Strategies for Making Concessions," https://hbswk.hbs.edu/item/four-strategies-for-making-concessions, in Harvard Business School Working Knowledge, March 6, 2006.

concession will be received more favorably if it is broken into installments.

Finally, avoid giving a concession without getting one in return. If you are asked for a concession, ask for something in exchange on the spot. Make your concession contingent on receiving one from them. For example, you could say "I could do X for you if you will do Y for me." If you do find yourself making a unilateral concession to get a stalled negotiation moving again, make sure you don't give another one until your counterpart concedes something to you. If you give two concessions in a row, your counterpart will ask for a third, and a fourth, and a fifth. If he understands that you will expect something in return for every concession you make, he will not be so quick to try his luck and ask for more. If he does ask, you might infer that it is important to him and consider whether you can agree to it (but don't forget to make it contingent on getting something in return).

Influence guru Robert Cialdini describes a persuasion technique he calls rejection-then-retreat.[*] It works because it is based on the concession principle.

First, make an excessive but not outrageous demand you fully believe your counterpart will reject. Your counterpart will almost certainly reject it. Then retreat to a more moderate position, which is what you actually wanted all along. By moderating your demand, you appear to be making a concession, which may very well result in a reciprocal concession in the form of compliance

---

[*] Described in detail by Robert B. Cialdini, *Influence: The Psychology of Persuasion* (1984).

with your modified request. This compliance technique is very hard to detect. I have heard it summarized like this: If you want a puppy, don't ask for a puppy—ask for a pony!

To summarize: Make your concessions sparingly, label them as having high value, break them into chunks, taper them as the negotiation progresses, and always ask for something in return for every concession you give.

Some negotiators believe you should never offer a currency or make a concession without getting something in return. Others believe that offering a unilateral concession can help advance a stalled negotiation. The first approach is sounder. If you feel tempted to make a concession to overcome an impasse, offer the concession in exchange for something else, for example, "I would be willing to offer X in exchange for Y."

If you do make a unilateral concession, do not make another concession without getting one in return. Two in a row will signal your counterpart to ask for more. Even small concessions have value and should not be given away freely.

OTHER TIPS FOR MAKING OFFERS AND COUNTER-OFFERS

- Do not appear too eager for a deal. If the other party senses you want it badly, she will make you pay a high price for it.

- Do not get emotional about the subject of the negotiation, for example, a house or a car. Remember, there are plenty of fish in the sea. Focus on your objective of getting what you want at a fair price and on good terms.

- Do not make a counter-offer too quickly. A counter-offer is a rejection of the previous offer. People take rejection personally. When the rejection is immediate and seemingly without careful consideration, it can be taken as a sign of disrespect. Take some time to think about every offer, especially when it is a complicated proposal rather than a simple price. People like their ideas to be taken seriously.

- Give reasons when making a counter-offer. Tell the other party what you like about their offer and what you would like to change, and why. People like to know why.

- Be prepared for any response, and control your reaction. You never know what the other party might say or do. Whatever the response, maintain your composure. Wear your poker face.

- Get offers and counter-offers in writing. Putting it in writing makes your offer seem more official and persuasive. People take written words and figures more seriously than spoken ones. Writing also protects against memory lapses, genuine or otherwise.

THE FLINCH

The flinch is another classic maneuver that we all expect. When done well, it works—even when we know the tactic is being used!

The flinch, or wince, is when you express shock or surprise at an offer. The intent is to send a message that the offer is shockingly unreasonable, in the hope that the offeror will retract his extreme offer and replace it with a more reasonable one. In this way, you get an immediate concession without making one yourself.

A flinch
- causes the offeror to have second thoughts about the fairness of his first offer;
- can help prevent an anchor from being set; and
- may cause the offeror to improve his offer before you respond.

There is no harm in trying the flinch, and it often works. But what should you do if your counterpart flinches in response to your opening offer? How do you counter a flinch? When your counterpart flinches, do not respond with a better offer right away. Instead, explain why you feel your offer is fair. Now you are discussing the offer, which legitimizes it and helps it to take hold as an anchor. Ideally, the other party would make a counter-offer rather than wait for you to unilaterally reduce your initial offer. If you choose to moderate your offer, your counterpart would have worked for it, and perhaps made a concession. You would not have made a unilateral concession.

I was at a neighborhood bazaar and saw a table of business books for sale. I noticed a particular title that I was interested in, and I knew that it cost about $30 in the bookshop. The book appeared pristine, but there was no price stated. I decided that if I could get it for less than $15, I would buy it. I asked the seller how much and he replied, "Five dollars." I blurted out, "Five dollars!" I was genuinely surprised at how cheap it was, but he thought I was flinching. Responding to my "flinch," he immediately said, "OK, three."

This not only illustrates the beauty of the flinch (even though it was unintentional), but also serves as an example of a good time to let the other party make the first offer. The seller did not know the value, so I got my pleasant surprise!

RELUCTANCE

I suggested earlier that you should never appear too eager for a deal. In a casual negotiation it pays to play it cool. When you express reluctance you are essentially playing hard to get. As in love, feigned disinterest often makes the suitor work harder to win you over. However, if it is obvious that the deal is important to you, pretending not to care can undermine your credibility. Show interest, but not desperation.

Imagine you are looking at a house for sale. Do you think the owner will bargain much if you exclaim, "This is my dream house! How much?" You would be better off explaining that you have seen a few houses that meet your needs and you are interested if the price is right. This implies that you have a Plan B (and you should have one in any serious negotiation) and are making a careful decision. They can't help you if they don't know what you want, but you don't want to appear needy.

THE SQUEEZE

You can often squeeze further concessions out of your counterpart without making a concession yourself simply by responding with a comment such as, "You'll have to do better than that" or "You need to go back and sharpen your pencil." You have told them their offer is unacceptable and they might try to improve it, but they do not know how much they must improve it. You're hoping for a pleasant surprise, that your counterpart may improve his offer beyond your expectations. If not, you can continue the negotiation from there—you haven't lost anything by trying.

What if your counterpart tries to put the squeeze on you? The counter-tactic to the squeeze is to reply "How much better?" Now, the squeezer is on the spot and needs to commit to a figure. You are not giving him the easy concession he was hoping for, and you are right back in the negotiation.

If you are the squeezer, anticipate the use of this counter-tactic and have a specific figure in mind. If it is not accepted, continue negotiating as before.

GOOD GUY/BAD GUY

You've seen this in the movies: the bad cop intimidates the suspect, then the nice cop comes in. The suspect confesses to the nice cop, thinking he will be better off dealing with a "friend." He focuses on the stylistic and personality differences between the good and bad guys, overlooking the fact that they are both on the same team and have the same objective.

This happens in business negotiations as well. The roles can be played by a team of negotiators, a businessman and his attorney, or even a husband and wife making a major purchase. It is an effective way of pressuring the other side into making bigger concessions.

Suppose a husband and wife are shopping for furniture. It is not practical for one person to be both interested and not interested at the same time, but if the wife is very interested in the dining room set and the husband is not ("Come on honey, let's look around ..."), the team has more flexibility to negotiate with the salesman or walk away.

The counter-tactic to the good guy/bad guy ploy is to expose the culprit. Let them know you are on to them and tell them you don't want to play games. Just say it in a good-natured way: "Oh, I get it, you're the good guy and you're the bad guy, right? Nice act! Now, are you serious about doing this deal?"

TIMING AS A TACTIC

Timing is an important element of any negotiation. Either party can slow down or speed up the pace of the negotiation to his advantage. Most negotiators overestimate their own pressures and weaknesses, while assuming their counterpart has a stronger position than she really does. You may feel that the clock is against you. This is because you are painfully aware of your own deadlines, sales targets, and other pressure points. You may not know what pressures your counterpart is under. Do not assume you have it worse than the other party. They may just be playing it cool—wouldn't you?

One party might impose a deadline to rush the other party to action. "The 50% off sale ends tonight. Tomorrow, this dining room set will go back to its usual price."

Or a party may drag his feet, hoping to prompt his counterpart into offering hasty concessions. "Well, I'm not sure, I'd like to think about it …"

Timing is a pretty intuitive matter to employ. You just know when it would serve you to speed things up or slow things down. On the other hand, it is not always easy to see when your counterpart is manipulating the clock, nor is it obvious how to handle it.

Here are a few things you need to know about timing tactics so that you can deal with them effectively:

- Everyone has a deadline, even if you don't know it. It may not be imminent, but you can't let any negotiation drag on forever.
- The party with the least time constraint has an advantage over the one with a tight deadline. If you have a tight deadline, you probably want to keep it to yourself. However, if you are close to a deal, you might let the other party know you have a tight deadline as it may pressure them into reaching an agreement.

Recall our discussion of leverage, or who has the upper hand at a given time (see Chapter 4). Leverage is largely a function of timing. The party who has time on their side has leverage, but the balance of power can change as time goes by—sometimes very quickly. Be aware of who needs a deal more at a given time, and continually reassess the situation as the negotiation progresses.

- Deadlines are usually arbitrary. They are set just to get you to act. You can always negotiate a change in a deadline. Even court and tax filing deadlines can be extended!
- The counter-tactic to a timing tactic is to do the opposite. If you feel pressure from a looming deadline, ask for more time. If your counterpart cites policy, ask to speak with a higher-up colleague. Explain that the negotiation is important, and both parties deserve adequate time to consider the merits. The dining room set will still be there in the morning. If you feel the negotiation is dragging on, impose a deadline yourself. Remind your counterpart that you have other alternatives, and need to decide by such and such a time.

Aside from time deadlines and delays, there are time scheduling issues to consider. You might be more focused in the morning than in the afternoon. You might not feel in the right mood for negotiating on a Monday morning, or you may be distracted by your weekend prospects on Friday afternoon. Your business— or your counterpart's—might be subject to weekly, monthly, seasonal, or annual cycles that could affect the negotiation. Holidays could also be a factor. Be aware of the impact these time factors could have on your negotiation and plan accordingly.

In many negotiations, most of the progress occurs in the final hours as the deadline approaches. This has two implications:

- Don't worry if you don't seem to be making much progress early in the negotiating process. This is normal. Continue asking questions, gathering information, exploring options, and bargaining. Remind yourself that huge divides can be closed in a short time as the clock runs down. It's all part of the game.
- You can manipulate and use deadlines to bring about progress. If you are in a rut, consider imposing a deadline to add a healthy dose of pressure.

COMPETITION

It's sometimes a good idea to casually let your counterpart know that you are talking with other parties and considering other alternatives. Let him know that he has competition, and that he will have to win your business. Remember, never appear too eager for a deal.

Competition takes many forms, and they may not be obvious. If you're looking to buy a car, other dealers are the obvious competition. The not-so-obvious competition might take the form of a bus card, a ride-sharing service, or an electric scooter.

Your counterpart also has alternatives, in the form of your competitors, obvious or not. Remind him of what makes you unique, whether it's your quality, reputation, experience, or some other differentiating factor. Remind yourself that he is negotiating with you for a reason.

AUTHORITY LIMITS

Whenever you negotiate, it's always a good idea to limit your authority. Having someone to check with is convenient when the other side is pressuring you for a commitment you may not want to make. Perhaps you are not as well prepared as you thought, or would like more time to think it over.

Car salesmen use this tactic all the time. After hearing your offer, they disappear to "check with their manager," then return to tell you their "hands are tied." You never get to see this invisible manager.

Many people let their egos get the better of them during a negotiation. They may say something like: "I'm the boss, I can do whatever I want, I don't need permission from anybody." Once you have said that, the other party may press you to agree to a proposal you may be unsure about.

But what if you really are the boss, and the other side knows it? There is no one higher whom you can defer to. So, what can you do? You can defer to someone lower than you. For example, you can say, "I'll have to check with my accountant before I commit to that figure," or "I need to run that past my marketing team and get back to you." As the boss, you delegate certain responsibilities to others you trust for their skill and judgment, and it is only natural to value and rely on their input.

Some negotiators like to ascertain at the beginning of the negotiation that they are dealing with a person with decision-making authority. This is good practice. However, if they try it with you, don't take the bait. Tell them you have authority to a point, and will need to check with others beyond that point. Do not name a specific person, or they may want to get his approval on the spot. Your higher authority should be a vague entity, such as a committee, management, or "my people."

Negotiations are unpredictable. Always leave yourself an exit. Even if you don't use it, you will be more comfortable—and confident—just knowing it's there.

SILENCE

There's an old axiom in sales: Whoever talks first loses. This is not always the case, but it usually is. Most people are uncomfortable with silence. During an awkward pause, they say something—anything—to break the tension. This is usually a mistake.

Learn to be comfortable with silence. Let the other party do the talking. She just might say something that is music to your ears.

Suppose your counterpart makes a concession. You remain silent. She is wondering what you're thinking, and might assume that you feel her concession is inadequate. As the silence becomes uncomfortable, she opens her mouth to speak—and offers you a bigger concession. She is now negotiating with herself.

If your counterpart clams up on you, don't give anything away. Repeat your last comment, ask her what she thinks about it, read through your papers, stare her in the eyes, or excuse yourself to make a phone call or use the restroom. Do anything to break the dynamic without conceding anything more. Just make sure you don't break into nervous giggles.

BUNDLING

You walk into a fast food restaurant for lunch. You order a burger and a medium drink. Then you notice that you can get the same burger and drink with fries for just a bit more. It seems like such a bargain. When you stop eating and stare at the remaining piece of burger and fries that you can't finish, you wonder why you ordered so much food. You've been bundled!

Sellers often bundle a set of related items at a special price to entice you to spend more. Sometimes it is a bargain, like when you really do want a burger, drink, and fries. Often, it is just a tactic to separate you from your money.

To counter the bundling tactic, focus on your interests. Determine which items in the bundle you want and which you do not want. Negotiate for a package that includes only what you want. Do not be swayed by a package of unnecessary extras just because it looks like a good deal.

HANDLING A TOUGH NEGOTIATOR

With all the lip service being paid to negotiating win-win outcomes in recent years, it is still not easy to get one. While we do see more of the collaborative style of negotiating that makes a win-win more likely, we often encounter a difficult or tough negotiator. How can we handle him and still get a good deal?

When facing a tough negotiator, you must first try to understand why she is being so difficult. Is she testing you? Is she playing hardball as a tactic? Is she in a bad mood (temper)? Or is she difficult by nature (temperament)? Once you identify the motive driving the difficult behavior, you can deal with it successfully.

Test

Some negotiators come on strong to see how you will react. They are hoping to intimidate you into giving up more than you would like. You need to hold your ground. If you stand up to them, you have passed the test and they will respect you. They may even tone it down a bit.

Tactic

Sometimes, the hard negotiator is being tough as a tactic. Even if you stand up to him, he will continue to push hard. He has learned through experience that he can often get a better outcome when he is more demanding, so he will try to wear you down. If this is his game, you must brace yourself and focus on what you want to get out of the deal.

The worst thing you can do with a tough negotiator is offer concessions in a misguided effort to appease him. You may be thinking that if you give in a little, he will appreciate it and ease up. But the message he will receive is that by being tough he is getting more, so he will continue to use the tactic—you have proven that it works! Each time your hard bargaining counterpart asks you for a concession, ask him for something in return. For example, you could say "I am willing to give you X if you will give me Y." Make him understand that there will be no free lunch.

Tests and tactics are rational behaviors. They are often employed by competitive style negotiators. Some negotiators, however, are difficult because of emotions.

Temper

Your negotiating counterpart may just be having a bad day. As a result, she may be hostile, irritable, or otherwise difficult to deal with. We have all had a bad day and let it affect the way we treat others.

If your counterpart is mistreating you because she seems upset about something, this could be a good time to ask the magic question: "Did I do anything to offend you?" If the answer is yes, you can ask what you did that caused offense, apologize for it, and continue to negotiate calmly. If the answer is no, it will become obvious to her that she has no reason to vent her anger at you and she will most likely calm down.

Temperament

There are a few people who simply do not play well with others. They may be arrogant, demeaning, unpleasant by nature, or just plain obnoxious. They are not testing you, playing hardball as a tactic, or just having a bad day—they are bullies. Perhaps your counterpart is abusive and enjoys wielding his power. You will not change him, but do not stoop to his level either. Take the high road and do your best. Be polite and professional. Stay focused on your objectives and work towards an agreement that satisfies him while meeting your own needs. A bully may not begrudge you your win as long as he gets what he wants.

The tough negotiator is a challenge in doing business. Rise to the challenge by understanding the reason for the behavior and addressing it.

CHAPTER 8

WRAPPING UP: CLOSING, IMPLEMENTATION, AND POST-NEGOTIATION MATTERS

"It ain't over 'til it's over."
—Yogi Berra

You've done your homework, asked questions and gathered information, identified interests and currencies, developed a Plan B, created value and options, and finally reached an agreement with your counterpart. You shake hands and congratulate one another on a job well done. Now what?

You feel relieved, exhilarated even. You look forward to enjoying the fruits of your efforts. Perhaps you feel so good that you don't even think about how those fruits will end up on your table.

Shaking hands over your agreement is not the end of the negotiation. Agreements don't implement themselves. There is still more to do!

ULTIMATUMS

Many negotiations end—with or without an agreement—after an ultimatum is issued. An ultimatum is a demand that something be done by a certain deadline, with a punishment for non-compliance. It is a threat that may or may not be believed by the recipient, and may or may not be carried out by the issuer. An ultimatum will often be delivered in a "Take it or leave it" or "Do it or else" form.

There are four ways in which an ultimatum can play out:

1. **Successful bluff**

   The issuer doesn't mean it, but the recipient believes it. The issuer got lucky.

2. **Failed bluff**

   The issuer doesn't mean it, and the recipient doesn't believe it. The issuer loses credibility.

3. **Successful ultimatum**

   The issuer means it, and the recipient believes it and concedes. The issuer gets his way without having to carry out his threat.

4. **Failed ultimatum**

   The issuer means it, but the recipient doesn't believe it. The issuer must follow through with the threat or risk losing credibility.

Does the issuer intend to
follow through with the threat?

	No	Yes
Yes Does the recipient believe the issuer will follow through with the threat? **No**	Successful Bluff	Successful Ultimatum
	Failed Bluff	Failed Ultimatum

This is a risky gambit. The result will depend in part on the resolve of the issuer and in part on whether the recipient believes the threat will be carried out. The issuer may be more or less convincing, but he cannot be sure how the recipient will respond.

When you say, "That's my final offer" or "Take it or leave it," you put yourself into a corner. If you follow through with your ultimatum, you may lose a deal you wanted. If you don't follow through, you lose credibility. Either way, you offend the other party. As credibility is so important and you cannot control how the other party may respond, you are better off not issuing an ultimatum unless you are fully prepared to follow through with it. Bluffing is risky!

If you must issue an ultimatum, make it a gentle one rather than a harsh one. "Take it or leave it" is abrupt and insensitive to the other party. He will be offended. You can convey the same either/or message in a much nicer way. For example, "It's the best I can do; work with me." This does not sound like an ultimatum; it sounds like a plea for help. The recipient will not be offended, and may even be sympathetic.

Give your ultimatum with a less desirable alternative, so your counterpart can choose. For example, "I know you could probably get your asking price eventually, but this is all we have in our budget." Notice you are still giving an ultimatum: take it (this is the best we can do) or leave it (you can try to get your price elsewhere), but it doesn't *sound* like an ultimatum. The recipient might not want to wait for a better offer, so your gentle ultimatum sounds like the better choice.

What should you do if your counterpart issues you an ultimatum? You have a few options:

- Offer a partial agreement on some terms and try to negotiate further on the others.
- Make a counter-offer. It is rarely either A (take it) or B (leave it). Offer them a new option C—they might accept.
- Ignore it and continue talking. Discuss other matters as a diversion and then come back to the negotiation: "Now, where were we? I believe your last offer was …" Or suggest they think about it and get back to you later. This reduces the pressure to follow through on their threat to maintain credibility and allows them a face-saving way to back down. The time buffer allows them to "forget" they issued an ultimatum. The more time that passes, the less likely they will follow through with their threat.
- Walk away (leave it), but be civil. Circumstances change, and you may find yourself back at the negotiating table with them later. Or you may exercise your Plan B.

DEALING WITH AN IMPASSE

You will frequently reach a point in a negotiation where you get stuck. Neither side wants to budge, progress is halted, and frustration mounts. You may wonder whether you will ever reach agreement. What can you do when you reach an impasse? Here are some suggestions:

1. Most progress in a negotiation usually occurs in the final stages. Recognize that an impasse is common and does not signal failure. Accept it as a hurdle that can and will be overcome.
2. Focus on your interests, and help your counterpart to focus on his. It is natural to get distracted by minor issues in the heat of bargaining. Refocusing on interests and priorities can get the negotiation back on track.
3. Look for creative ways to add value. Explore options that have been overlooked. As a negotiation proceeds, you learn new information that can lead you to other possible solutions.
4. Offer to grant a small concession, but demand one in return. A small movement can get things rolling again.
5. Focus the negotiation on smaller or easier items. As you reach agreement on some minor points, you build momentum that can carry you forward.
6. Change the dynamics of the negotiation. A change in players and personalities can jumpstart a stalled negotiation.
7. You might also change the environment. Different surroundings can change the atmosphere and put you back on track.
8. Take a time out. Review your strategy and allow emotions to cool down. Sometimes, taking a break to relax and clear your head can work wonders.

WRAPPING UP: CLOSING, IMPLEMENTATION, AND POST-NEGOTIATION MATTERS   211

9. Agree to impose a period of silence. This is not the same as taking a break. Everyone stays in the room, they just don't say a word for five or ten minutes. During this time, all kinds of thoughts creep into our minds, causing both sides to moderate their expectations.

10. You could also impose a deadline. In many negotiations, most of the progress is made in the final stages, as the deadline approaches. Sometimes, time pressure is just the kick in the pants the parties need to get things moving again.

11. Ask your counterpart for his agreement. Sometimes it is just as simple as asking. If he says yes, great! If he says no, ask why not? Listen carefully to his answer, address his concerns, and set forth the remaining steps needed to conclude an agreement.

12. If things seem hopeless, consider bringing in an impartial third party. More often than not, a good mediator can help the parties to reach an agreement.

13. Finally, be prepared to walk away if necessary. Just be sure you are not bluffing, and that you have someplace to walk away to. This takes guts, but it may apply pressure on the other side to be more flexible.

An impasse need not be the end of the line. Be persistent and you can put the negotiation back on track.

MEMORANDA AND DRAFT AGREEMENTS

It's important to take careful notes throughout the negotiation. Whether you are meeting face to face or negotiating over the phone, take notes. You'd be surprised how often you and your counterpart forget things, or have different recollections of things discussed. Your notes will come to the rescue. You may even find that what you and the other party actually agreed to is more favorable to you than what you recalled.

People forget things. Even with the best of intentions, we cannot remember everything. Taking notes makes you more attentive to the negotiation, which is reason enough for taking notes, but it is also a good idea to protect yourself at every stage of the process. If the negotiation is complicated or takes place over a long period of time, draft a memorandum from your notes periodically to reflect the current state of affairs. In any event, you will certainly want a final memorandum at the end of the negotiation. This memorandum may even be the basis for what will become a formal written agreement.

I suggest that you draft any written contract yourself. Your counterpart may genuinely appreciate that you have taken responsibility for this, although that is not the main reason for doing it. You and your counterpart will inevitably have different understandings about what you are agreeing to, and you will prefer to make your understanding the basis of the final agreement. As you draft the contract, you will naturally shape it according to your understanding. This does not mean you have devious motives; you probably won't even be aware of it. Chances are your counterpart won't be aware of it either.

Some negotiators like to draft an agreement before they even begin negotiating! This may sound premature, but the idea has merit. It forces you to think about what you really want to get out of the negotiation. It also gives you a chance to set high aspirations. While the final agreement will probably look different than what you conceived earlier, your first draft gives you something to measure the final agreement against. Compare the proposed final agreement with this earlier draft before you finalize it to make sure you didn't overlook anything important.

Your counterpart may also wish to write the contract. If so, read it over carefully. Make sure it conforms to your understanding as reflected in your notes. If anything seems amiss, raise the issue with the other party immediately.

As you haggle over the final terms you may have a series of revisions to make or approve. Do not focus only on the red pencilled changes when comparing drafts. Check all subsequent revisions as carefully as the first draft.

Lawyers spend an inordinate amount of time and charge hefty fees for poring over contracts. It is often worth the extra time and expense.

IMPLEMENTING THE AGREEMENT

Have you ever made plans to meet a friend, only to find that the meeting never takes place?

"Where were you? You were supposed to meet me last night!"

"No, we discussed it, but you never called back to confirm it."

"But I thought we had agreed to meet. I didn't think we needed to reconfirm."

It seemed like a simple enough plan at the time, but the two of you had different understandings.

Agreements don't implement themselves. People implement agreements and people sometimes misunderstand, forget, or fail to follow through.

Any written contract should make clear the who, what, when, where, and how of the agreement. If there is only an oral agreement, your notes or memos should reflect the parties' understanding. Follow up to make sure both parties are doing what they agreed to do.

Remember the two sisters who squabbled over the orange? They eventually discovered that one wanted to squeeze out the juice, while the other wanted to grate the rind to make a cake. The solution sounds simple enough in theory, but it may not be so simple to execute. Will the thirsty one squeeze out the juice first, and give her sister a messy peel afterwards? Or will the baker grate the rind first, and give her sister a nearly naked and hard to squeeze fruit? When do they each plan on using the parts they need? While they may think their problem was solved, their troubles may not be over yet!

I mentioned earlier that it is wise to draft an agreement before you begin negotiating. At the very least, ask yourself: what will the final agreement look like? Continue to think about this over the course of the negotiations. Ask yourself:

- What steps must be taken? By whom? By when?
- What possible obstacles might arise? Potential misunderstandings? How might you avoid them?
- How can you help your counterpart "sell" the agreement to his constituents?
- How will the agreement be monitored?

At the end of the formal negotiation, after the final handshake, you will want to celebrate and stop thinking about all the details of the agreement. As time goes by, these details become a blur. You move on to other projects. You assume the deal will happen as planned.

To avoid problems later, make sure the final agreement provides detailed answers to the questions above. At the very least, assign the follow-up work to a particular person who will be held accountable, such as your personal assistant. Provide a clear framework for implementing the agreement.

NIBBLES

A nibble is a last-minute attempt by one party to grab an extra concession from his counterpart. For example, a car buyer might ask the salesman to throw in a set of new floor mats, or a home buyer might ask the seller to include certain appliances not already included in the contract.

A nibble is a consciously employed tactic, not the afterthought it seems to be. The nibbler knows the other party may be feeling generous while basking in the afterglow of a successful negotiation, and he tries to take advantage of this goodwill. Or perhaps the party being nibbled may fear the deal will fall through if he doesn't agree to this relatively minor request. Not wishing to appear petty, he agrees.

A nibble is especially effective after the other party has invested substantial time, effort, or psychic energy in the negotiation. However, your counterpart will probably resent it. She may feel that you are greedy or you are not negotiating in good faith.

Like all tactics, there is also a counter-tactic to the nibble. In fact, there are several. Let's look at them here:

- First, you might make it contingent. A nibble is a request for a concession, and we do not like to make unilateral concessions. Defend against the nibble by saying "I might be able to give you that, if you can give me this."

- You can defer to higher authority. "I'd love to give you those floor mats, but my manager would never agree to it."

- If you are in a business where you get the same kind of nibble all the time, put a price on it. "Let's see, according to our standard price list, I can give you that set of new floor mats for only $189. Shall I add that to the purchase order?" People can say anything, but a written price list is the type of authority people don't usually argue with.

- You can appeal to fairness. "Come on now, I've already given you such a good deal. I really can't give you any more."

- You can let the nibbler know you're onto his game. "Hey, that was a pretty good nibble!" The nibble is designed to seem casual and not look like a tactic. The tactic doesn't work when the veil is stripped off. Be very careful with this—you don't want to cause the nibbler to lose face when exposing him. Unless you know the person well, consider using one of the other four defenses above.

POST-SETTLEMENT SETTLEMENTS

A post-settlement settlement (PSS) is a settlement that is agreed to after the parties reach their initial agreement. It is not a second, unrelated agreement, but an improved version of the first agreement. It allows you to leverage on your success and do even better.

A post-settlement settlement sounds like an oxymoron. Why would you want to settle an agreement that has already been settled? The very idea sounds suspect, which may be why these devices are so rarely used, and are often viewed with suspicion when they are proposed. However, a PSS can be a great way to improve an already good deal.

Your initial agreement may not be as good as it could have been. You didn't know the other party that well, and may not have built enough trust to share information as fully as you could have. You may not have thought of all of the currencies or addressed all of the interests. You may have accepted a good deal too quickly for fear of losing it, rather than holding out for a better deal. After the dust settles, you think of ways you could have done better. Or maybe you can't think of any particular improvements you would like to make, but you would like to explore further possibilities.

A PSS can create additional value for both parties. The fact that you have reached an agreement shows that you can work with your counterpart. You have built up trust and goodwill, and you have helped one another become better off than you were before you reached your agreement. You both took risks in negotiating and those risks paid off. With this track record of success in joint problem solving, you are both confident that you can continue to help one another do even better.

A PSS assumes that the initial agreement will remain in effect if the parties are unable to reach a better agreement. You can continue to negotiate with your initial agreement serving as your new Plan B. It is also your counterpart's Plan B. Both of you must do better (or at least be no worse off) than your initial agreement or you will not agree to change it. You have nothing to lose by considering a PSS.

For example, suppose you negotiate an employment package with a new employer. Your agreement states that you will begin your employment in 30 days, which allows you to give the requisite notice to your current employer. Your current employer unexpectedly agrees to waive that requirement and lets you go at the end of the week. The prospect of sitting at home without pay for the next three and a half weeks does not excite you, so you call your new employer and ask to re-examine the timing issue. If she would like you to begin immediately, you are both better off. Otherwise, you both stick to your original agreement.

You might be reluctant to raise the idea of a PSS because of what your counterpart might think. He might think you are having second thoughts about the agreement and are trying to back out or extract more concessions from him. He might wonder why you think you could reach a better agreement now—were you not negotiating in good faith earlier? Did you learn something new? Did your situation change? These thoughts do not inspire confidence that your agreement will work out as expected.

It is natural for someone not familiar with the PSS concept to have these doubts. You need to anticipate and overcome them. How you raise the matter is important. Emphasize that you are happy with your agreement and intend to honor it. Explain that there might be ways to improve it, and that you would like to explore some ways if they are mutually advantageous. Ask whether your counterpart has similar thoughts, or is at least open to the possibility of improving the agreement.

The fact that the initial agreement—the new Plan B for both parties—guarantees that neither party will be worse off if there is no PSS should make you and your counterpart comfortable in exploring new and better possibilities.

WHEN THINGS GET UGLY: LITIGATION, MEDIATION, AND ARBITRATION

There will be times when you and your counterpart fail to reach an agreement where failure is not an option (for example, a management-labor negotiation), or you disagree about a provision in an agreement you made earlier. In times like these, one party may break off the negotiations with the words, "I'll see you in court!"

Aside from extreme measures such as war, strikes, and lockouts, there are three methods for resolving breakdowns in negotiations: litigation, mediation, and arbitration.

Litigation
Glamorized in movies and on TV, litigation is the most familiar means of resolving a dispute. The idea is simple: the parties go to court to see who has the better lawyer!

The wheels of justice turn slowly, and it is very expensive to keep the machinery going. A judge decides the matter, which is subject to appeal and additional investments of time, energy, and, of course, money. In the end there is a winner and a loser, or possibly two losers after all the legal bills have been paid.

In addition to the long time frame and high expense, litigation has other drawbacks. The outcome is uncertain and beyond the control of the parties—it is very risky. People in business like to reduce risk, not expose themselves to it. Litigation is a public process, and the decision is usually a matter of public record. Most people don't like airing their dirty laundry in public. The decision is handed down by a judge (or possibly a jury). While a judge may be an expert on the law, he may not be that knowledgeable about the substance of the dispute— there may be people who are more qualified to settle the matter. Finally, the confrontational nature of the legal process usually destroys whatever relationship the parties may have enjoyed. Litigants often choose a tough lawyer to make the other side pay. Unfortunately, highly confrontational lawyers are not always the best medium for resolving disputes amicably.

For these reasons, there is a growing trend in many jurisdictions to require parties to first attempt to resolve their dispute by other means. When the parties arrive in court for their pre-trial hearing, the judge will ask them if they have tried mediation. If they haven't, he will say, "Go down the hall to room 2-C and spend an hour with the mediator." As the impact of the uncertainty of the outcome and exorbitant expense of litigation sinks in, the parties usually find that they can agree to a settlement after all.

Of course, you don't have to wait for the judge to send you to mediation. You and your counterpart can agree to mediation or arbitration before either party decides to litigate. Going to court is a serious and expensive matter, with dire ramifications for your relationship. It should be used only as a last resort. In fact, the overwhelming majority of lawsuits are settled out of court.

Mediation

Mediation is a less formal process than litigation. The rules of evidence and procedure are greatly relaxed, and lawyers are optional. It is quick and inexpensive. There is no judge; rather, an impartial third party tries to facilitate an agreement between the disputing parties. The parties can choose to reach an agreement or not; no decision is imposed upon them. However, the mediator's skill in negotiation and dispute resolution, combined with her people skills, can often help the parties to overcome their differences and reach a win-win solution.

The beauty of mediation is its win-win philosophy. The parties are usually emotional and looking to beat their counterpart. (Remember, they may have been on their way to court a few minutes earlier.) Their attorneys are trained to be adversarial and are looking to justify their fees by giving their client a resounding victory, and perhaps destroying their opponent in the process. However, the mediator is trained to look for win-win solutions that others may have overlooked. She is often able to help the parties reach an amicable agreement, or at least an acceptable compromise. The provisions of the agreement are confidential. The parties may well leave the room on good terms, their relationship intact.

Arbitration

Like mediation, arbitration is a relatively quick, inexpensive, and informal alternative to litigation. However, there are a few important differences. The arbitrator, or the panel of arbitrators, is usually an expert in the field. For example, in a dispute between a general contractor and a subcontractor in a construction matter, the arbitrators may have experience in engineering, construction, or project management. They are better able to understand the intricacies of the dispute and can render a more informed decision than a judge.

Unlike mediation, the arbitrator's decision is usually binding. The parties agree to submit their case to an expert and abide by his decision, rather than take their chances with a judge. In fact, many contracts provide that disputes will be submitted for arbitration rather than litigation. There is usually no appeal from an arbitrator's award. As with mediation, the decision is private and the parties' relationship may well survive the proceedings.

Of the three methods of dispute resolution, mediation is most useful in keeping with the spirit of a win-win negotiation. In fact, mediation *is* a form of negotiation, with the guidance of an expert. Avoid litigation and the specter of a lose-lose result if at all possible.

* * * * * *

There is much more to learn about becoming a win-win negotiator. No doubt you will learn some lessons from the mistakes you will make. Remember that doing so is infinitely better than *not* learning from your mistakes. Take heart in the knowledge that even world class negotiators make mistakes. Becoming a win-win negotiator is a life-long journey, but it is a rewarding one.

POSTSCRIPT: THE FUTURE OF NEGOTIATION

Negotiation has been around since the dawn of mankind. People have always cooperated and competed, and negotiation is part of both. For much of the history of business, competitive win-lose negotiating was the norm. You have something I want, but I want to get as much as I can for as little as possible. I'll use tactics and dirty tricks to do so, and you'll try to protect your interests with counter-tactics and more dirty tricks. People haven't changed much in all these thousands of years, and neither has the practice of negotiation.

The biggest change in the way negotiation is practiced has been the principled or win-win approach advocated by Professor Roger Fisher and his colleagues. The emphasis on joint problem solving, preparation, expanding the pie, differentiating positions and interests, empathy, and relationships was exactly what we needed in the last two decades of the 20th century. The business environment was changing dramatically:

- Information technology and the Internet made information more widely available, leveling the playing field and creating legions of savvy buyers in both the consumer and commercial realms.

- Technological complexity and specialization changed the way we work, with more democratic corporate structures and collaboration needed to integrate knowledge, skill, and expertise.

- Companies still competed but were more likely to cooperate as well, with a proliferation of joint ventures, strategic alliances, partnerships, and co-branding arrangements requiring unprecedented levels of collaboration.

None of these forces will go away. In fact, information accessibility, complexity and specialization, and the centrality of relationships will continue to have increasing impact on the way we live and do business. There are also newer forces coming into the mix as well:

- The generations that are now coming of age are not willing to play by the same rules as the boomers and their predecessors. They measure success differently. Money often takes a back seat to other currencies, such as purpose and causes bigger than themselves, for example, the environment, meaningful experiences, and making a difference.

- The circle of stakeholders will continue to expand. Management, labor, shareholders, vendors, and customers are being joined by voices speaking on behalf of residents, whales, and trees. Those voices will become louder and more diverse.

Environmental, social, and governance measures are becoming more important relative to the bottom line.

- Social media makes it very risky for companies, governments, and other actors to engage in sharp practices that previously might have had little consequence. And everyone will be able to find their tribe.

- The gig economy means a lot of workers who never thought about negotiating now have to think about it and practice it in their role as CEO—Chief Everything Officer.

My friend Avi told me a beautiful story. He had hired Sandeep, a solopreneur web designer who was just starting out, to build his website. They agreed on a price and the scope of work and Sandeep set out to do the job. After Avi saw the finished website, he called Sandeep and said, "I don't think I can pay you the agreed price for your work."

"What do you mean you can't pay?" Sandeep replied. "I did everything you asked for. We had a deal …"

"I understand we had a deal, but your work has exceeded my expectations. You deserve more than what we agreed. I'd like to pay you an additional 20%."

"What? Wow! Are you serious? I really appreciate that, but you don't have to pay me anything extra."

"Yes, I do. You deserve it. I want to be fair with you."

The amount in question was not a large sum, but Sandeep was delighted. Not only did he get a pleasant surprise and a bonus, he also felt valued. When Avi's website was hacked, Sandeep fixed it without charge.

Sandeep's business has grown, and he has raised his fees. Avi has hired him to build a couple more websites for him, and has also referred several new customers to Sandeep. But Sandeep charges Avi less than his other customers, and he still gives Avi his personal attention. Their business relationship is straightforward and characterized by trust and goodwill. Both give their best and know that they are being fairly treated by each other. And they have become good friends.

Tactics, secrecy, positional bargaining, and the competitive mindset will never go away, but they will become less common. Relationships, interest-based problem solving, and the win-win mindset will continue to grow in importance. The win-win negotiator is just hitting his stride.

THE WIN-WIN NEGOTIATOR'S CHECKLIST

1. **Distinguish Interests vs Positions**
   To uncover your true interests, ask yourself *why* it is important to you.
   What are your *real* interests? Prioritize them.
   What are your counterpart's interests?
   Are there any other stakeholders whose interests should be considered?

2. **Identify Currencies—anything of value**
   What do you have that your counterpart values?
   What do they have that you value?
   What currencies can you leverage to create value?
   Consider differences in perception, timing, risk tolerance, intangibles, emotional needs, etc.

3. **Generate Options—packages of currencies, possible solutions**
   What options would best satisfy my interests? Their interests?
   Look for creative solutions.
   How can I create more options using a variety of currencies (including intangibles)?

4. **Develop a Plan B**
   List all the alternatives you can think of, and the pros and cons of each.
   Which alternative is most favorable? Is it realistic?
   Can you improve it?

What is your best estimate of your counterpart's Plan B? How can you minimize it?

5. **Rationale—an external, objective standard for evaluating possible outcomes**

What possible rationales can you come up with? Fairness is important.

Prioritize standards—which are most advantageous to you? To your counterpart?

How can you help your counterpart sell it to his boss/ stakeholders?

6. **Communication**

Build rapport, empathize, be likable.

Ask lots of questions.

Listen carefully.

Consider cultural issues.

7. **Relationship**

Separate the people from the problem.

Seek to understand your counterpart, see their point of view.

Keep emotions in check.

8. **Implementation—promises and agreements about what each party will do**

What do you hope to accomplish?

What will the final agreement look like?

Minimize your risks—use guarantees, deposits, contingency provisions, milestone payments, etc.

Be clear about follow-up actions—who is supposed to do what, by when?

Include dispute resolution procedures.

ABOUT THE AUTHOR

David Goldwich practiced law in the US for more than a decade. Recognizing that lawyers perpetuate rather than solve problems, he has since reformed and hasn't sued anyone in years.

David has taught negotiation and other business topics at the tertiary level in the US and in Singapore. He speaks internationally and conducts workshops and seminars in negotiation, storytelling for leaders and sales professionals, business presentations, assertiveness, and leadership. An engaging and provocative speaker, David uses humor and stories gathered from his own experience as a lawyer, businessman, and father to help people reach breakthrough changes in their personal and professional lives. He is the author of four other books: *Kickass Business Presentations: How to Persuade Your Audience Every Time, Win-Win Negotiations: Developing the Mindset, Skills and Behaviours of Win-Win Negotiators, Getting into Singapore: A Guide for Expats and Kaypoh Singaporeans,* and *Why Did the Chicken Cross the Road?: Lessons in Effective Communication,* and hundreds of articles.

Born and raised in Miami, Florida, David has been living in Singapore and working throughout Asia since 1999. He enjoys art, music, stock investing, the beach, red wine, chocolate, and anything Italian.